BANGKOK

TRAVEL GUIDE 2025

*Your Essential Companion to Discovering
Dynamic Street Markets, Historic Temples,
and Immersive Thai Culture and Experiences.*

Cedric J. Stone

COPYRIGHT

To Get More of My Books, Kindly Scan The QR Code.

TABLE OF CONTENTS

Gratitude

Dear Readers,

Thank you for choosing this book to guide you on your next adventure. Your interest and curiosity are greatly appreciated, and I am grateful for the chance to share the beauties of our world with you. Before you begin the adventures detailed within these pages, I'd like to express my heartfelt gratitude.

Your support means everything to me, and I am confident that this book will be a valuable companion on your journey. Whether you're planning your first vacation or returning to uncover new treasures, you'll find inspiration, practical insights, and a greater bond with the places you visit.

Enjoy every second of your journey, and may your memories be as breathtaking as the sights you will see.

Thank you for your participation in our adventure.

BANGKOK, THAILAND MAP

SCAN ME

HOW TO SCAN THE QR CODE

1. Open your smartphone's camera or QR code scanner app.
2. Point the camera at the QR code.
3. Wait for the camera to recognize the code.
4. Tap the notification or link that appears.
5. Follow the link or instructions provided.

INTRODUCTION

Welcome to Bangkok

Bangkok, Thailand's bustling capital, is a city that wears many hats—an urban metropolis steeped in tradition, a culinary capital, and a dynamic cultural hub where East meets West in unexpected ways. Known locally as *Krung Thep Maha Nakhon*, this "City of Angels" enchants visitors with its intricate blend of ancient temples, sleek skyscrapers, charming street life, and a nearly infinite option of experiences for every kind of traveler.

From early morning markets to late-night street food stalls, Bangkok's rhythm is unmissable, and its charm lies in its contrasts. Stroll along the historic *Chao Phraya River* and witness a world where centuries-old Buddhist temples sit side-by-side with ultra-modern malls, each vying for attention in the cityscape. This seamless blend of old and new is Bangkok's signature, creating a city that feels both timeless and endlessly evolving.

Yet, Bangkok's true charm lies in its layers of experience. It's a city that invites exploration, rewarding travelers with hidden gems, distinct neighborhoods, and moments of tranquility amid the excitement. Whether it's exploring the luxury shopping malls in Sukhumvit, meandering through the historic Old City, or relaxing in the green spaces of Lumphini Park, Bangkok offers an endless array of discoveries.

Quick Facts about Bangkok

To make the most of your Bangkok adventure, a few essentials are worth keeping in mind. Here's a brief rundown to get you prepared:

- **Population**: Approximately 10 million.
- **Language:** The official language in Bangkok is Thai, though English is widely spoken in tourist areas.
- **Currency:** Bangkok's official currency is the Thai Baht (฿). ATMs are everywhere, and credit cards are widely accepted in larger establishments.

- **Time Zone:** GMT+7, with no daylight saving adjustments.
- **Weather:** Bangkok's tropical climate is hot and humid, with three main seasons: Hot (March–June), Rainy (July–October), and Cool (November–February).
- **Electricity:** 220V AC, 50 Hz, with types A, B, and C plugs.
- **Getting Around:** Bangkok's main airport, Suvarnabhumi International (BKK), is a modern hub connecting the city to the world. The city's extensive BTS Skytrain and MRT systems, along with its iconic river ferries, make getting around convenient.

For first-time travelers, remember to bring comfortable clothing suited to warm weather, a good pair of walking shoes, and a sense of adventure. It's also handy to learn a few basic Thai phrases; simple greetings and courtesies go a long way in connecting with locals.

Why Visit Bangkok in 2025?

Bangkok in 2025 is a city where tradition meets innovation, creating an experience unlike any other. Imagine stepping into a world where gleaming skyscrapers tower over ancient temples, and the bustling city streets come alive with the aromas of sizzling street food and the hum of vibrant markets. This year, Bangkok offers visitors even more reasons to come explore, as the city embraces a surge of new developments in hospitality, eco-conscious tourism, and immersive cultural experiences.

With the reimagined riverside at *ICONSIAM*, new sustainable initiatives in the green sanctuary of *Bang Krachao*, and the electrifying return of festivals like *Songkran* and *Loi Krathong*, Bangkok's spirit feels more alive than ever. It's a place where every street corner tells a story, from the intricate artistry in *Wat Phra Kaew* to the hidden lanes of *Yaowarat's Chinatown*, where old-world charm mingles with the modern hustle and bustle.

But beyond the sights, it's the warmth of the people that captivates. The Thai people's hospitality makes you feel part of something larger, offering a sense of community that draws you in, whether you're bargaining in *Chatuchak Market* or sharing a quiet moment on a *Chao Phraya riverboat* at sunset. With more eco-friendly travel options, sustainable hotels, and a flourishing food scene that caters to every palate and budget, Bangkok in 2025 isn't just a destination—it's a journey of cultural discovery, culinary exploration, and connection.

So why visit Bangkok in 2025? Because there's a pulse to this city, a rhythm that calls out to both the curious and the seasoned traveler, offering memories that linger long after you leave. Bangkok is ready to welcome you, to surprise you, and to make you feel like you've found a home halfway across the world.

Whether you're a first-time visitor or a seasoned traveler, the "City of Angels" offers something new to uncover with each visit.

How to Use This Guide

Welcome to the ultimate Bangkok travel guide, crafted to make your experience in this dynamic city both memorable and meaningful.This guide has been thoughtfully crafted to help you make the most of your time in Bangkok, whether you're here for a day, a week, or longer. Inside, you'll find everything you need—from practical tips to insider recommendations—organized to make planning as enjoyable as the trip itself.

Start by exploring the "Planning Your Trip" section in Chapter One, which covers the best times to visit, visa information, and budgeting tips, setting a strong foundation for your journey. Then, explore the "Getting to Bangkok" and "Getting Around Bangkok" chapters, which offer advice on navigating Bangkok's bustling streets, from airports to public transportation.

For travelers eager to explore, head to the "Bangkok's Must-See Attractions" chapter for iconic sights and hidden gems. Our in-depth neighborhood guides in the "Top Neighborhoods and Areas" section will help you get a feel for each area's unique vibe. For those who crave adventure and want tailored experiences, the chapter on "Suggested Itineraries" offers a variety of options, including family-friendly plans, romantic getaways, and itineraries for nature lovers.

Bangkok is also a culinary haven, so don't miss the section on "Dining in Bangkok" to discover top restaurants, budget-friendly spots, and must-visit food markets. As the sun sets, the "Nightlife and Entertainment" section will guide you to the best bars, nightclubs, and traditional performances for an unforgettable evening.

Finally, we've included essential resources like "Practical Travel Information" and "Sustainable and Responsible Travel" to keep you safe, prepared, and conscious of your environmental impact. Also, the "Useful Apps, Resources, and Contacts" chapter wraps up the guide with key tools and contacts to ensure you have all the support you need.

This guide isn't just about places; it's about experiences. Let it be your companion, offering you the heart and soul of Bangkok. Dive in, explore with curiosity, and let Bangkok captivate you.

CHAPTER ONE

Planning Your Trip

Planning your trip to Bangkok is the first step in uncovering the wonders of this enchanting city. From the best times to visit and visa requirements to budgeting and travel tips, this chapter will prepare you for an unforgettable journey through Thailand's enchanting capital. Bangkok has something magical to offer year-round, whether it's dynamic festivals, the blissful calm of temples, or bustling markets that light up the night., but knowing when to go and what to expect will ensure you make the most of every moment.

Best Times to Visit

Bangkok's tropical climate brings warm temperatures and high humidity all year, but the city experiences three primary seasons: cool, hot, and rainy. Each season has its own appeal, but knowing what to expect can help you choose the best time to visit based on your preferences and activities. Here's a breakdown of each season to help you decide the best time for your trip:

Cool Season (November to February)

The cool season is the most popular time to visit Bangkok, offering pleasant temperatures between 20–30°C (68–86°F) and lower humidity. This is ideal for outdoor activities, temple visits, and river cruises. The city's energy is high during the cool season, with festivals like *Loy Krathong*, where locals release floating lanterns on rivers, and the enchanting Chinese New Year celebrations. However, because this is peak tourist season, hotels, flights, and attractions are relatively pricier. Booking accommodations and flights in advance will help you secure better deals and availability. Despite the crowds, this season offers the ideal mix of pleasant weather and festive energy.

Hot Season (March to June)

Bangkok's hot season brings intense heat, with temperatures frequently reaching 35–40°C (95–104°F). While the heat can be intense, it's also a great time to enjoy the city's indoor attractions like museums, art galleries, and air-conditioned shopping malls. The famous Thai New Year, *Songkran Festival*, occurs in April, where locals and visitors alike join in a city-wide water fight to cool down from the heat. If you plan to visit during this time, stay hydrated and wear light, breathable clothing to beat the heat.

Rainy Season (July to October)

Bangkok's rainy season is marked by sudden downpours and humid conditions, with temperatures ranging from 25–30°C (77–86°F). Although rain can be unpredictable, it usually comes in short bursts, and you can still explore the city with minimal interruption. This period is also excellent for budget-conscious travelers, as hotels and flights are more affordable, and fewer tourists mean shorter queues at major attractions. Traveling during the rainy season can be rewarding with some flexibility and an umbrella on hand. If you're willing to embrace the occasional shower, Bangkok's sights are equally beautiful under moody, rain-washed skies.

In summary, while November to February offers the most comfortable weather, each season has its perks, making Bangkok an appealing destination year-round.

Visa Requirements and Entry Tips

Understanding Thailand's visa requirements is essential to ensure a smooth arrival in Bangkok. Thailand offers various visa options depending on your nationality and the length of your stay, so let's go over the basics:

Visa-Exempt Countries

Citizens from several countries, including the United States, the United Kingdom, Canada, Australia, and most European nations, can enter Thailand without a visa for up to 30 days if you are arriving by air or up to 15 days if arriving by land. This exemption is great for short-term travelers, but be sure to have a valid passport with at least six months remaining before expiration and proof of onward travel. However, confirm entry requirements as policies can change.

Tourist Visa (Single and Multiple Entry)

For travelers planning to stay longer, Thailand offers a Tourist Visa valid for 60 days, which can be extended for an additional 30 days. This visa is available as a single entry or multiple-entry visa, the latter being beneficial if you intend to explore neighboring countries and return to Thailand. Tourist visas can be obtained from Thai embassies or consulates in your home country before departure, and the process typically requires proof of funds, return flights, and accommodation.

Visa on Arrival

Travelers from select countries can obtain a Visa on Arrival (VOA) for a stay of up to 15 days. The VOA is issued at select entry points, including Bangkok's main airports, and typically requires proof of sufficient funds, an onward ticket, and a valid passport. Be prepared to pay the visa fee in cash (Thai Baht only). Additionally, check Thailand's Ministry of Foreign Affairs website before departure, as requirements can change.

Digital Nomad and Special Tourist Visas

With Bangkok becoming popular among digital nomads, Thailand has introduced a Special Tourist Visa (STV) and other long-term visa options, which allow stays of up to 90 days, extendable for up to 270 days. These visas cater to those interested in longer stays and are worth considering if remote work or extended exploration is your goal.

Entry Tips

When entering Thailand, immigration officials may ask to see proof of onward travel, such as a return or onward flight ticket. It's also recommended to have the address of your first accommodation in Bangkok on hand, as this can sometimes be required. To avoid any delays, ensure your passport has at least two blank pages for stamps and is valid for at least six months from the date of entry.

Before traveling, always confirm the latest visa requirements for your nationality, as regulations may change. It's also wise to carry a printed copy of your flight details and accommodation reservation, as these may be requested upon arrival.

Budgeting and Travel Costs

Bangkok is a versatile city that can cater to luxury seekers, budget travelers, and everyone in between. Knowing what to budget for helps you enjoy Bangkok's treasures without surprises. Here's a rough guide to budgeting for different aspects of your trip:

Accommodation

Bangkok offers a wide range of accommodation options. Budget travelers can find clean, comfortable hostels and guesthouses starting from 300 THB per night, while mid-range hotels typically range from 1,000 to 2,500 THB per night. Luxury travelers can expect to spend 3,000 THB and upwards for high-end hotels with all the amenities, including pools, spas, and city views.

Food and Dining

One of Bangkok's greatest appeals is its affordable and delicious food. Street food meals cost as little as 30-60 THB, making it easy to enjoy Bangkok's culinary scene without breaking the bank. For a sit-down experience in a local restaurant, expect to pay around 100-300 THB per meal, while fine dining at upscale restaurants ranges from 1,000 THB and above per person.

Transportation

Bangkok's extensive transportation options make it easy to get around on a budget. A one-way BTS Skytrain or MRT subway ride typically costs between 16 and 59 THB. Taxis and tuk-tuks are widely available but negotiate the fare in advance or ensure the meter is used. Grab (a ride-hailing app) is another convenient option. Riverboats are also an affordable way to travel, with fares starting around 10-30 THB, and they offer a unique view of the city.

Activities and Attractions

The cost of attractions in Bangkok is generally affordable, with temple entry fees around 100-500 THB and museum visits ranging from 100 to 200 THB. For a mid-range budget, a daily expense of 1,500-2,500 THB covers meals, transportation, and basic sightseeing comfortably.

Daily Budget Estimates

- **Budget Travelers**: 1000- 1700 THB per day.
- **Mid-Range Travelers:** 2000–3400 THB per day.
- **Luxury Travelers:** 5000 THB per day.

With affordable options in food, transport, and accommodations, Bangkok is an accessible city for any budget. Planning your finances will help you enjoy the best of Bangkok, whether you're seeking budget-friendly thrills or high-end experiences.

CHAPTER TWO

Getting to Bangkok

Bangkok is one of Southeast Asia's busiest travel hubs, welcoming millions of visitors each year through its well-connected international airports. As a gateway to Thailand's diverse experiences, from bustling city life to serene temples and tropical islands, Bangkok has developed an efficient system for incoming travelers. Understanding your arrival options, navigating customs, and knowing how to get to your hotel from the airport are essential for a smooth start to your trip.

Major Airports and Arrivals

Bangkok has two main airports: *Suvarnabhumi Airport (BKK)* and *Don Mueang Airport (DMK)*. Both serve international and domestic flights, though they cater to different types of airlines and travelers.

Suvarnabhumi Airport (BKK)

Often referred to as Bangkok's main international gateway, Suvarnabhumi Airport is one of the largest airports in Southeast Asia and a major hub for international travel. Located about 30 kilometers east of downtown Bangkok, BKK handles the bulk of international flights, including those operated by major carriers such as Thai Airways, Emirates, Qatar Airways, and Singapore Airlines. The airport is modern and well-equipped with facilities like restaurants, currency exchange services, lounges, and duty-free shopping.

Don Mueang International Airport (DMK)

Known as Bangkok's secondary airport, Don Mueang primarily serves low-cost airlines like

AirAsia, Nok Air, and Lion Air, making it a popular choice for budget-conscious travelers. Located about 24 kilometers north of central Bangkok, Don Mueang mostly handles regional and domestic flights, though it also operates some international routes. While smaller and less modern than Suvarnabhumi, Don Mueang is efficient, and its manageable size means shorter walking distances and potentially quicker check-ins.

When booking flights to Bangkok, travelers often choose Suvarnabhumi for international connections and Don Mueang for domestic or budget-friendly regional flights. Each airport has efficient customs processes and transportation options, making either choice convenient depending on your travel plans.

Navigating Customs and Transportation Hubs

Clearing customs in Bangkok is generally a straightforward process, especially if you're prepared with the right documents and knowledge of arrival procedures. Here's what to expect when navigating customs and accessing transportation hubs at both airports:

Passport Control and Entry Requirements

After disembarking, head to *passport control,* where you'll present your passport and completed arrival card (usually provided on the plane). Ensure that your passport is valid for at least six months and that you have a printed copy of your onward or return ticket, as immigration officers may request proof of departure.

Customs and Immigration

Once you disembark from your flight, follow signs for immigration. Bangkok's airports are well-marked in English, so it's easy to find your way. For international arrivals, you'll go through immigration, where you'll need to present your passport and completed arrival card (usually provided on the plane). Most visitors receive a 30-day visa exemption (depending on nationality), while others may need a visa on arrival. Once cleared, collect your luggage from the designated carousel and head toward customs. You'll see two channels: the green channel for those without anything to declare and the red channel for those with items to declare. Be aware that random checks can occur, so have your belongings organized.

Currency Exchange and ATMs

Both Suvarnabhumi and Don Mueang have currency exchange counters and ATMs available in the arrivals area. While exchange rates are generally fair at the airport, ATMs offer a convenient alternative, though a withdrawal fee often applies. It's a good idea to have a small amount of Thai Baht (THB) on hand for transportation and immediate needs.

SIM Cards and Connectivity

Staying connected in Bangkok is easy, with various options for SIM cards available right at the airport. Major providers like AIS, TrueMove, and Dtac have kiosks in the arrivals area, offering prepaid SIM cards with data packages tailored for tourists. These plans often include unlimited data and local calling options, making it simple to stay connected from the moment you land.

Luggage Services

If you have heavy luggage or need temporary storage, Bangkok's airports offer baggage services and luggage storage facilities. You can store items for a few hours or several days, depending on your needs.

Transportation Hubs

Each airport is well-connected to various transportation options, including taxis, buses, shuttles, and trains, allowing you to reach Bangkok's city center or other destinations easily. Both airports provide clear signage in English, and information desks are available for additional assistance.

Getting from the Airport to Your Hotel

Once you've cleared customs and collected your luggage, you'll find several ways to get from the airport to your accommodation in Bangkok. Choosing the right option depends on your budget, convenience, and whether you prefer a private or public mode of transportation.

Suvarnabhumi Airport (BKK) to City Center

Airport Rail Link (ARL)

The Airport Rail Link is one of the most efficient ways to travel from Suvarnabhumi to the city center, especially during peak traffic hours. Running every 10-15 minutes from early morning until midnight, the ARL connects Suvarnabhumi directly to central Bangkok with stops at major transit hubs, including Phaya Thai (BTS Skytrain) and Makkasan (MRT). The entire journey to Phaya Thai takes about 30 minutes, with fares ranging from 15 to 45 THB (about $0.50 to $1.50 USD).

Taxi Services

Taxis are widely available at Suvarnabhumi, with a designated taxi queue outside the arrivals area on the ground floor. The fare to central Bangkok typically ranges from 250 to 400 THB ($7 to $12 USD), plus a 50 THB airport surcharge and any applicable toll fees. Make sure the taxi meter is operating or negotiate and agree on a price before starting your journey. Taxis are ideal for travelers with heavy luggage or those arriving late at night when public transportation is less accessible.

Ride-Hailing Apps (Grab)

Grab, Southeast Asia's popular ride-hailing service, operates at Suvarnabhumi, providing a convenient alternative to traditional taxis. Fares vary by destination and time, but Grab offers the advantage of pre-calculated rates and cashless payment. Grab is especially useful for first-time visitors who prefer a hassle-free experience with clear fare visibility.

Private Transfers and Hotel Shuttles

Many hotels in Bangkok offer private airport transfers that can be arranged before arrival, providing a comfortable and stress-free option. Additionally, several companies offer private transfer services, which can be booked online or at the airport. Prices for these services typically start around 800 THB ($25 USD) and increase depending on vehicle type and distance.

Don Mueang Airport (DMK) to City Center

Airport Shuttle Bus to Mo Chit BTS

Don Mueang offers a shuttle bus service connecting to Mo Chit BTS station, the nearest Skytrain station, making it easy to continue to your destination via Bangkok's BTS network. The shuttle operates regularly, and the trip to Mo Chit is approximately 20 minutes, depending on traffic. From Mo Chit, you can access other parts of Bangkok by switching to the BTS.

Taxi Services

Like Suvarnabhumi, Don Mueang has a designated taxi area where licensed taxis are available. A trip to central Bangkok usually costs around 200 to 350 THB ($6 to $10 USD), plus a 50 THB airport surcharge and possible toll fees. As always, ensure the taxi meter is turned on to avoid any misunderstandings about fares.

Ride-Hailing Apps (Grab)

Grab is also available at Don Mueang, making it convenient for travelers who prefer a cashless, pre-calculated fare. Simply order your ride through the app and meet your driver at the designated pickup zone.

Public Buses

For budget-conscious travelers, Don Mueang Airport has public buses connecting to various areas of Bangkok. The A1 and A2 bus routes are popular choices, with stops at major transportation hubs like Chatuchak Park (MRT) and Mo Chit (BTS). These buses are an economical choice, with fares starting at 30 THB (under $1 USD), although travel time can vary depending on traffic.

Pro Tips for a Smooth Arrival

- **Keep Essential Documents Accessible:** Make sure to keep your passport, arrival card, hotel reservation, and any necessary travel documents handy for a swift check-in at immigration.

- **Pre-download Maps:** Bangkok is vast, and having offline maps downloaded can help you navigate more easily, especially if you need directions to your hotel.

- **Prepare for Traffic:** Bangkok's traffic can be unpredictable, so if you're heading to a specific appointment or meeting, allow extra travel time, especially if you're taking a taxi.

- **Stay Hydrated:** Thailand's warm climate can be a surprise for first-time visitors, so keep a bottle of water with you, particularly after a long flight.

With a little preparation, your arrival in Bangkok will be smooth and stress-free, allowing you to start your adventure in this incredible city the moment you touch down. From the airport to your hotel, Bangkok offers a range of efficient, affordable, and comfortable transportation options that make navigating the city easier than ever.

CHAPTER THREE

Getting Around Bangkok

Navigating Bangkok is an adventure in itself, with a variety of transportation options that let you experience the city from different perspectives. From the efficient BTS Skytrain to the lively tuk-tuks, getting around Bangkok is part of the journey. Here's what you need to know about the city's transport options and some insider tips for a smooth experience.

Public Transportation: BTS, MRT, and Buses

Bangkok's public transportation system is well-developed, making it easy to travel across the city efficiently and affordably. Below is a closer look at this facet:

BTS Skytrain

The BTS Skytrain, or simply the BTS, is one of Bangkok's fastest and most convenient transportation options. It has two main lines (Sukhumvit and Silom) that cover major business, shopping, and entertainment districts. Operating from around 6:00 a.m. to midnight, the BTS is air-conditioned, clean, and perfect for avoiding Bangkok's notorious traffic. Fares range from 16 to 59 THB ($0.45 to $1.70), depending on the distance.

MRT Subway

The MRT subway complements the BTS, covering areas the Skytrain doesn't reach. With two lines (Blue and Purple), the MRT connects key neighborhoods and intersects with the BTS at various points, making transfers easy. Like the BTS, the MRT is air-conditioned and operates from 6:00 a.m. to midnight. Fares are similar, ranging from 16 to 42 THB ($0.45 to $1.20), depending on distance.

Buses

Bangkok's buses are the most budget-friendly but can be a bit challenging for non-Thai speakers. Routes are extensive and cover the entire city, with fares ranging from 8 to 25 THB ($0.20 to $0.70) depending on the type of bus (regular or air-conditioned). Though slower than the BTS or MRT due to traffic, buses provide an authentic experience and are great for exploring local neighborhoods. Apps like *ViaBus* can offer guidance on route planning.

Tuk-Tuks, Taxis, Ferries, and Ride-Sharing Apps

For a more personal and often thrilling ride, Bangkok offers a variety of street-level transport options.

Tuk-Tuks

These three-wheeled vehicles are a Bangkok icon. Brightly colored and open-air, tuk-tuks offer a fast (sometimes hair-raising!) way to zip through the city. Fares are negotiable and should be agreed upon before starting the journey, as tuk-tuks don't have meters. Expect to pay around 100–300 THB ($3–$9)

for a short ride, depending on distance and traffic. Tuk-tuks are best for short journeys or when you're in the mood for a unique, local experience.

Taxis

Taxis in Bangkok are affordable and plentiful. Most have meters, but it's important to ask the driver to use it before the trip starts. Flag drop fares start at 35 THB ($1), and most rides within the city center cost around 60–150 THB ($1.70–$4.30), depending on traffic and distance. Avoid rush hour if possible, as traffic can be intense. Note that some drivers might prefer cash only, so keep small bills on hand.

Ferries and River Taxis

Bangkok's *Chao Phraya River* is lined with many of the city's most famous attractions, and ferries are a scenic way to reach them. Public ferries operate along the river with fares starting at 15 THB ($0.40), depending on the route. Tourist boats, with higher fares around 50 THB ($1.40), also offer hop-on, hop-off options for convenient sightseeing. Ferries are an enjoyable way to travel, providing picturesque views and a chance to escape street traffic.

Ride-Sharing Apps

Apps like *Grab* (similar to Uber) are widely used in Bangkok and offer a convenient alternative to traditional taxis. Grab offers transparent, upfront pricing and cashless payment options, which many travelers find convenient. It's also great for those unfamiliar with Thai, as drivers follow app-based directions to your destination.

Travel Tips: Traffic, Safety, and Etiquette

Getting around Bangkok can be enjoyable with a few travel tips to ensure a smooth experience:

- **Traffic:** Bangkok's traffic is infamous, especially during rush hours (8:00–10:00 a.m. and 4:00–7:00 p.m.). If you're on a tight schedule, it's best to rely on the BTS, MRT, or express boats to avoid delays. Alternatively, plan ample time if taking a taxi during peak hours.

- **App Recommendations**: Apps like Google Maps, Grab, and Moovit can be invaluable for navigation, fare estimation, and understanding transportation routes. The BTS and MRT also have their own apps with schedules, fare information, and service updates to make travel easier.

- **Negotiating Fares**: *Tuk-tuks* and some taxis may try to negotiate fares. For tuk-tuks, always agree on the price before starting your journey. For taxis, insist on using the meter; if a driver refuses, it's best to wait for another taxi.

- **Safety:** Bangkok is generally safe, but always be cautious with valuables in crowded areas, like markets or public transport. Keep bags close and use hotel safes for important documents. When taking a tuk-tuk or motorbike taxi, hold onto your belongings tightly, as the open design can make items easy to lose.

- **Etiquette:** In public transport, respect local customs by offering seats to monks, elderly, and pregnant women. Avoid loud conversations and observe basic etiquette, especially in places like the BTS and MRT where silence is appreciated. When interacting with drivers, a polite greeting and a smile go a long way, and it's customary to thank them with "Khop khun kha" (for women) or "Khop khun krap" (for men) after your trip.

From the sleek efficiency of the Skytrain to the bustling vibe of tuk-tuks, Bangkok's diverse transportation options add layers to your experience, revealing the city's character from different angles.

CHAPTER FOUR

Top Neighborhoods and Areas

Bangkok is a city of dynamic contrasts, where traditional culture thrives alongside modern urban life. Each district has its own unique vibe, offering visitors a blend of experiences, from ancient temples and riverside views to bustling nightlife and trendy cafés. Here's an in-depth look at some of Bangkok's most popular districts, where you can immerse yourself in everything this distinct city has to offer.

Old City (Rattanakosin): Heritage Sites and Culture

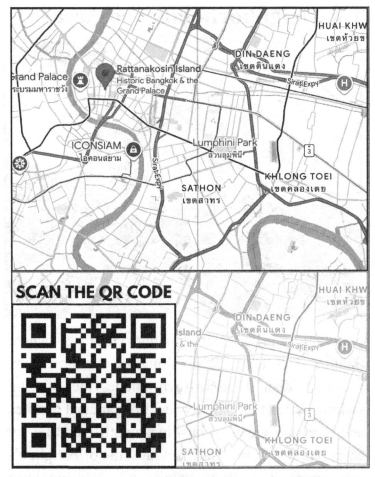

SCAN THE QR CODE

The Old City, or "Rattanakosin", is Bangkok's cultural and historical heart, home to the city's most famous landmarks and a treasure trove of Thai history. Known for its traditional architecture, heritage sites, and proximity to the Chao Phraya River, the Old City is a must-visit for those interested in Thailand's rich cultural fusion.

Top Attractions

The Grand Palace and Wat Phra Kaew

The Grand Palace and Wat Phra Kaew (Temple of the Emerald Buddha) are the jewels of the Old City, showcasing intricate architecture and revered religious artifacts. Just a short walk away is *Wat Pho*, famous for its giant reclining Buddha and traditional Thai massage school. *Wat Arun*, across the river, is also a stunning sight, especially at sunset when the temple's porcelain façade glows in the light.

Dynamic Local Markets

Don't miss the opportunity to visit *Pak Khlong Talat*, Bangkok's largest flower market. This colorful marketplace is open 24/7 and offers an incredible array of flowers and produce, often at very affordable prices. It's a sensory experience that gives visitors a feel for local life in Bangkok.

Historic Neighborhoods

Walking through Rattanakosin, you'll find historic neighborhoods with traditional wooden shophouses, art galleries, and Thai handicrafts shops. The area around Khao San Road, while known for its backpacker-friendly nightlife, is also home to quaint alleys filled with cafes, craft shops, and street food.

- **Cultural Tips:** Rattanakosin is Bangkok's cultural soul, so be mindful of local customs, especially when visiting temples. Dress modestly, cover your shoulders and knees, and avoid loud conversations. The Old City embodies Bangkok's heritage and is a place for reflection and respect.

Sukhumvit: Modern Bangkok and Nightlife

Sukhumvit is Bangkok's dynamic, cosmopolitan hub, known for its skyscrapers, high-end malls, international restaurants, and an electrifying nightlife scene. This district offers a glimpse of Bangkok's fast-paced modernity, where Thai and international influences merge seamlessly.

SCAN THE QR CODE

Shopping and Dining

Sukhumvit is famous for its luxury malls, with *Terminal 21* and *EmQuartier* being popular spots for both locals and tourists. Terminal 21's unique theme of international cities, with each floor representing a different global destination, makes it a fun shopping experience. Meanwhile, EmQuartier is known for its upscale boutiques and rooftop dining with stunning views of the city.

Diverse Nightlife

Sukhumvit's nightlife caters to every taste, from glitzy rooftop bars to quirky pubs and renowned clubs. Soi 11, in particular, is packed with popular bars and clubs like Levels and Havana Social, where you'll find a mix of tourists and locals enjoying Bangkok's distinct nightlife. For a more laid-back experience, check out rooftop bars like Octave at the Marriott Hotel, offering panoramic views of the city skyline.

Cultural Diversity

Sukhumvit is also known for its multicultural vibe, especially around areas like Phrom Phong, which hosts the city's Japanese community, and Asok, which has many Middle Eastern and Indian restaurants. This makes it a fantastic spot to explore diverse cuisines and cultures within Bangkok.

Getting Around

The BTS Skytrain runs directly through Sukhumvit, making it easy to navigate. The stations provide access to many popular sites, dining areas, and malls, allowing visitors to explore the district effortlessly.

Riverside: Scenic Views and Iconic Attractions

Bangkok's Riverside area along the Chao Phraya River is a mix of historical landmarks, luxury hotels, and scenic views. The Riverside has a slower, more relaxed vibe than other districts, making it a popular choice for those seeking a serene experience with some of the city's most iconic attractions nearby.

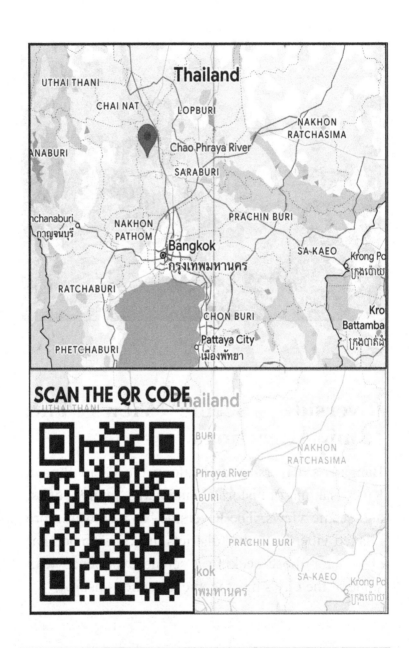

SCAN THE QR CODE

Historic Sites and Temples

The Riverside area is close to some of Bangkok's most celebrated cultural sites, including Wat Arun, the Grand Palace, and Wat Pho, all easily accessible by river ferries. Taking a ferry along the river is an experience in itself, offering scenic views of temples, markets, and traditional wooden houses on stilts.

Luxury Hotels and Fine Dining

The Riverside is home to some of Bangkok's most prestigious hotels, including the Mandarin Oriental,

Shangri-La, and The Peninsula. These hotels offer luxury amenities, fine dining, and beautiful riverside views. Many also have renowned restaurants, such as The Verandah at the Mandarin Oriental, which serves international cuisine in a charming riverside setting.

River Cruises and Night Markets

Evening cruises on the Chao Phraya River are a popular activity, with options ranging from budget-friendly public ferries to lavish dinner cruises with Thai performances and international buffets. *Asiatique The Riverfront*, a night market and open-air mall, is a must-visit for shopping, dining, and live entertainment along the water.

Photography Opportunities

Riverside Bangkok is a photographer's dream, offering stunning views of Bangkok's skyline against the serene Chao Phraya River. Sunset is the perfect time to capture the beauty of the temples and riverboats with the cityscape as a backdrop.

Thonglor and Ekkamai: Trendy Bars and Cafés

Thonglor and Ekkamai, neighboring areas located on Sukhumvit's eastern stretch, are Bangkok's trendiest neighborhoods, popular with the city's young, creative crowd. Known for their stylish bars, chic cafés, and upscale restaurants, these districts offer a taste of Bangkok's contemporary lifestyle and social scene.

Unique Cafés and Restaurants

Thonglor and *Ekkamai* are packed with unique and Instagram-worthy cafés, such as the rustic Blue Whale Café, which serves up ocean-inspired blue lattes, and Toby's, known for its stylish

Australian-inspired brunch menu. Here, you'll find everything from traditional Thai food to international fusion, crafted with a modern twist.

Bars and Nightlife

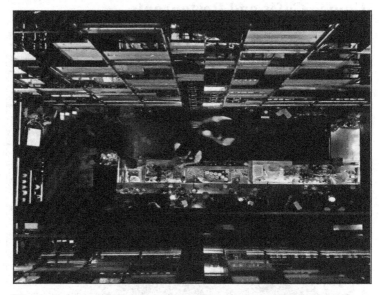

Thonglor and Ekkamai come alive at night, with a range of bars, speakeasies, and clubs. Places like Rabbit Hole and Iron Balls Distillery offer innovative cocktails in stylish, intimate settings, while Beam nightclub caters to electronic music fans with an impressive sound system and a sleek, industrial vibe. These neighborhoods attract a mix of locals, expats, and visitors looking for a night out in a trendy, cosmopolitan setting.

Boutique Shopping

Thonglor and Ekkamai are also home to unique boutiques and concept stores, where you'll find fashion, home décor, and local designer brands. The Commons, a multi-level lifestyle space in Thonglor, offers a collection of boutique shops, cafes, and eateries in a community-oriented setting, perfect for leisurely shopping or relaxing with friends.

Art and Design

Art galleries and design spaces are also common in Thonglor and Ekkamai, catering to the creative community that thrives in this area. Many galleries showcase contemporary Thai artists, adding a dynamic cultural dimension to these trendy neighborhoods.

Whether you're exploring the cultural landmarks of the Old City, the nightlife and shopping in Sukhumvit, the riverside charm, or the hip scenes of Thonglor and Ekkamai, each of Bangkok's districts offers its own unique slice of city life. Embracing the diversity of these neighborhoods allows travelers to experience Bangkok from multiple perspectives, making every day in the city a fresh and exciting adventure.

CHAPTER FIVE

Where to Stay in Bangkok

Bangkok's accommodation scene is as diverse as the city itself, offering a range of options for every budget and travel style. From luxurious riverside resorts to trendy mid-range hotels, affordable hostels, and unique eco-lodges, Bangkok caters to everyone. Here's a curated list of some of the city's best places to stay, complete with price ranges in Thai Baht and USD, convenient details on location, and the facilities you can expect to help you make the perfect choice for your trip.

Luxury Resorts

For travelers seeking a luxurious escape, Bangkok's high-end resorts offer refined elegance, world-class service, and spectacular amenities that promise an unforgettable stay. Here are five of the most popular luxury resorts in Bangkok:

Mandarin Oriental Bangkok

Why stay here?

The Mandarin Oriental combines Thai heritage with world-class luxury. Overlooking the Chao Phraya River, this iconic hotel offers spacious rooms with river views, two swimming pools, a fitness center, and a variety of restaurants, including the renowned *Le Normandie. The Oriental Spa* and Thai cooking school add a traditional touch to this lavish experience.

- **Location:** 48 Oriental Avenue, Charoenkrung Soi 40.
- **Price Range**: 20,000–50,000 THB ($570–$1,425) per night.
- **Facilities:** Spa, riverside pool, fine dining restaurants, personal butler service, fitness center.
- **Nearby Attractions**: Close to the Temple of the Reclining Buddha, the Grand Palace, and easy access to Asiatique Riverfront Night Market.

The Peninsula Bangkok

Why stay here?

The Peninsula is a luxurious riverside hotel located along the Chao Phraya River, offering stunning views of Bangkok's skyline. Known for its elegant design and world-class service, this five-star property features spacious rooms and suites with Thai-inspired decor and modern amenities. Guests can enjoy a variety of dining options, including Thai, Chinese, and international cuisine, as well as a renowned riverside bar.

- **Location:** 333 Charoennakorn Road, Klongsan.
- **Price Range:** 14,000 – 25,000 THB per night ($390 – $695 USD).
- **Facilities:** Features luxurious rooms with panoramic river views, a three-tiered pool, and a riverside spa. Guests can enjoy a private boat shuttle across the river and dine at the award-winning Mei Jiang Cantonese restaurant.
- **Nearby Attractions:** Located near IconSiam mall, Wat Arun, and close to BTS Saphan Taksin Station for city access.

Banyan Tree Bangkok

Why stay here?

The Banyan Tree is a luxurious, high-rise hotel in the heart of Bangkok, Thailand, known for its exceptional service, elegant accommodations, and breathtaking city views. Located in the Sathorn/Silom area, the hotel offers easy access to Bangkok's bustling shopping districts, dynamic nightlife, and cultural landmarks. One of its standout features is the *Vertigo and Moon Bar*, a rooftop dining and bar experience on the 61st floor, providing panoramic views of the city skyline and Chao Phraya River.

- **Location:** 21/100 South Sathon Road.
- **Price Range:** 10,000 – 30,000 THB ($280 – $850 USD) per night.
- **Facilities**: The Banyan Tree offers a stylish stay with luxury spa treatments, an outdoor pool, and dining options that range from authentic Thai cuisine to international fare. The spacious suites have floor-to-ceiling windows, providing stunning city views.
- **Nearby Attractions:** Close to Lumphini Park and CentralWorld Mall, with easy access to the Silom and Sathon districts.

Park Hyatt Bangkok

Why stay here?

The Park Hyatt is a luxurious five-star hotel located in the heart of Bangkok's dynamic Central Embassy district. Known for its sleek, modern design and striking architecture, the hotel combines Thai cultural elements with contemporary elegance. It offers stunning views of the Bangkok skyline from its infinity pool and features sophisticated dining options, including the Penthouse Bar + Grill, which is popular for its panoramic city views and lively atmosphere. With its spacious rooms, world-class spa, and convenient proximity to upscale shopping and cultural landmarks, Park Hyatt Bangkok provides a tranquil yet stylish escape in the bustling capital.

- **Location:** 88 Wireless Road, Pathum Wan.
- **Price Range:** THB 10,000 – 20,000 per night ($275 – $550 USD).
- **Facilities:** This sleek hotel features a rooftop pool, fitness center, and several fine-dining options. The rooms are stylish and offer expansive views of the Bangkok skyline.

- **Nearby Attractions:** Adjacent to Central Embassy Mall, near BTS Phloen Chit station, and walking distance from Lumpini Park.

Anantara Riverside Bangkok Resort

Why stay here?

The Anantara Riverside Resort is a luxurious riverside retreat set amidst lush tropical gardens along the banks of the Chao Phraya River in

Bangkok. This resort seamlessly blends Thai heritage with modern elegance, offering guests a peaceful escape from the city's bustling energy. With spacious rooms, multiple dining options—including the renowned Trader Vic's and Riverside Terrace—alongside a stunning infinity pool overlooking the river, the resort provides both relaxation and cultural immersion.

- **Location:** 257/1-3 Charoennakorn Road, Thonburi.
- **Price Range:** 12,000–30,000 THB ($340–$860) per night
- **Facilities:** Features a large outdoor pool, lush gardens, and an array of dining options, including the famous Trader Vic's. The resort offers a serene retreat with activities like river cruises and a Thai cooking class.
- **Nearby Attractions:** Accessible by boat to the Grand Palace and Wat Arun, with easy access to Asiatique Night Market.

Mid-Range Options

These mid-range hotels provide excellent comfort, convenient locations, and great value for travelers looking to enjoy Bangkok without breaking the bank. Here are five of the most popular Mid-Range accommodation options in Bangkok:

Adelphi Suites Bangkok

Why stay here?

The Adelphi Suites is a modern, stylish hotel located in the dynamic Sukhumvit area of Bangkok, known for its lively shopping, dining, and nightlife scene.

This hotel offers spacious, apartment-style suites equipped with kitchenettes, making it ideal for both short and extended stays. Guests enjoy easy access to the Nana BTS Skytrain station, which is just a short walk away, providing convenient connectivity to the rest of the city. The hotel features a rooftop pool with city views, a fitness center, and an on-site restaurant, *Monsoon Café*, popular for its Thai and international dishes.

- **Location:** 6 Sukhumvit Soi 8, Khlong Toei.
- **Price Range**: 2,500 – 4,500 THB per night ($70 – $125 USD).
- **Facilities:** Adelphi Suites offers spacious, modern rooms with kitchenettes, making it ideal for longer stays. Guests enjoy a rooftop pool, a fitness center, and an on-site restaurant.
- **Nearby Attractions:** Situated in Sukhumvit near BTS Nana Station, close to Terminal 21 and Central Embassy Mall.

The Quarter Phrom Phong

Why stay here?

The Quarter Phrom Phong is a stylish and contemporary hotel located in the dynamic Phrom Phong district of Bangkok, Thailand. Known for its modern design and prime location, it's an ideal base for travelers looking to explore the city's bustling shopping, dining, and entertainment scene. The hotel is just a short walk from the *BTS Phrom Phong Station*, providing easy access to popular attractions around Bangkok. Guests enjoy amenities such as a rooftop pool with panoramic city views, a well-equipped fitness center, and spacious, elegantly designed rooms.

- **Location:** 31 Sukhumvit Soi 39.
- **Price Range:** 2,000 – 4,000 THB per night ($55 – $110 USD).
- **Facilities:** Features contemporary rooms, a rooftop pool, and a gym. It also offers a free shuttle service to nearby BTS stations and malls.
- **Nearby Attractions:** Near Emporium Mall, EmQuartier, and Benjasiri Park, with easy access to Sukhumvit nightlife.

Novotel Bangkok Sukhumvit 20

Why stay here?

The Novotel Bangkok Sukhumvit 20 is a modern, upscale hotel located in the dynamic Sukhumvit district, one of Bangkok's most popular areas for shopping, dining, and nightlife. This hotel offers a blend of comfort and style with well-appointed rooms, a rooftop infinity pool with sweeping city views, and a variety of dining options, including *Food Exchange* for international cuisine and *Sky on 20,* a rooftop bar with panoramic views.

- **Location:** 19/9 Soi Sukhumvit 20, Khlong Toei.
- **Price Range:** 2,800 – 5,000 THB per night ($75 – $140 USD).
- **Facilities:** Features a rooftop infinity pool, fitness center, and multiple dining options, including a rooftop bar with city views.
- **Nearby Attractions:** Walking distance to Asoke BTS and Sukhumvit MRT, close to Terminal 21 and Benjakitti Park.

Casa Nithra Bangkok

Why stay here?

The Casa Nithra is a charming boutique hotel located in the heart of Bangkok, offering a blend of modern comfort and traditional Thai elegance. Known for its warm hospitality and stylish decor, the hotel provides cozy, well-appointed rooms and facilities like a rooftop pool, where guests can relax while enjoying views of the city skyline. Its convenient location near popular attractions, such as *The Grand Palace* and *Khao San Road,* makes it ideal for travelers wanting to explore Bangkok's cultural landmarks. Casa Nithra is popular for its relaxing ambiance, combining urban convenience with a touch of Thai heritage.

- **Location:** 176 Samsen Road, Phra Nakhon.
- **Price Range:** 1,500 – 3,000 THB per night ($40 – $85 USD).
- **Facilities:** Features stylish rooms and a rooftop pool, blending traditional Thai décor with modern amenities.
- **Nearby Attractions:** Close to Khao San Road, the Grand Palace, and the lively Rattanakosin district.

Hotel Muse Bangkok

Why stay here?

The Hotel Muse is a luxurious boutique hotel that seamlessly blends vintage charm with contemporary sophistication. Located in the heart of Bangkok's upscale Langsuan neighborhood, it offers easy access to dynamic shopping districts, cultural landmarks, and nightlife. Each room is beautifully designed with Art Deco and European-inspired interiors, creating an atmosphere of timeless elegance. The rooftop bar, Speakeasy, provides stunning city views and a fantastic ambiance, making it a favorite spot for both guests and locals.

- **Location:** 55/555 Langsuan Road, Lumphini.
- **Price Range:** 3,000 – 5,500 THB per night ($85 – $155 USD).
- **Facilities:** Known for its 1920s European-inspired decor, Hotel Muse offers elegant rooms, a rooftop bar, a pool, and a fitness center.
- **Nearby Attractions**: Located near Central Chidlom, Lumphini Park, and BTS Chidlom Station.

Budget-Friendly Lodgings

Bangkok's budget accommodations are perfect for travelers looking to save while still enjoying comfort and cleanliness. Here are five popular budget-friendly accommodations in Bangkok:

Here Hostel Bangkok

Why stay here?

Here Hostel is a dynamic, social, and stylish accommodation set in the heart of Bangkok's old town, just a short walk from Khao San Road. Known for its chic design and welcoming atmosphere, Here Hostel offers travelers a unique experience with cozy dorms, private rooms, and a playful twist—a slide from the second floor straight to the lobby! It's the perfect spot for meeting fellow travelers, relaxing in hammocks in the garden, or exploring nearby landmarks like the Grand Palace and Wat Pho. With its combination of comfort, fun, and location, *Here Hostel* is a fantastic choice for backpackers and social explorers alike

- **Location:** 196/3-8 Ratchadamnoen Road, Bovornnivet, Phranakorn.
- **Price Range:** 500 – 1,200 THB per night ($14 – $35 USD).
- **Facilities:** Features clean, cozy dorms and private rooms with a shared pool and bar, making it a great social spot for travelers.
- **Nearby Attractions:** Close to Khao San Road and the Grand Palace.

Lub d Bangkok Silom

Why stay here?

Lub d Bangkok Silom is a social hostel located in the heart of Bangkok's bustling Silom district. Known for its lively atmosphere, stylish design, and budget-friendly accommodations, it's the perfect spot for travelers looking to meet new people and explore the city. With cozy dorms, private rooms, and shared spaces like a chic lounge and co-working area, Lub d offers a comfortable and trendy base for discovering Bangkok. Plus, it's just a short walk from top attractions, street food markets, and public transport, making it easy to dive into the city's endless adventures!

- **Location:** 4 Decho Road, Suriyawong.
- **Price Range:** 600 – 1,500 THB per night ($17 – $42 USD).
- **Facilities:** Offers dorms and private rooms, a bar, co-working space, and a travel desk.
- **Nearby Attractions:** Close to BTS Chong Nonsi, Lumpini Park, and the dynamic Silom area.

The Yard Hostel Bangkok

Why stay here?

The Yard Hostel is a trendy, eco-friendly oasis in the heart of the city's dynamic *Ari neighborhood.*

Known for its welcoming vibe and social atmosphere, this unique hostel offers guests a sense of community with cozy common areas, lush outdoor gardens, and creative events. Guests can relax in stylish private rooms or dorms built from repurposed shipping containers, blending comfort with sustainability. The Yard is an ideal spot for travelers looking to meet new friends, explore Bangkok's local cafes and markets, and experience a peaceful retreat within the bustling city.

- **Location:** 51 Phahonyothin Road, Ari.
- **Price Range:** 400 – 1,000 THB per night ($11 – $28 USD).
- **Facilities:** Eco-friendly and community-focused, Features dorms and private rooms, a garden area, and a bar.
- **Nearby Attractions:** Near Ari BTS station, surrounded by local eateries and cafes.

New Siam III Guest House

Why stay here?

New Siam III Guest House is a budget-friendly accommodation located in the heart of Bangkok's dynamic Banglamphu district. Situated just a short walk from the bustling Khao San Road and the serene Chao Phraya River, it offers guests a convenient base to explore the city's rich cultural landmarks. The guest house features clean, air-conditioned rooms equipped with essential amenities, ensuring a comfortable stay for travelers. Guests can enjoy complimentary Wi-Fi, a 24-hour front desk, and an on-site restaurant serving a variety of Thai and international dishes.

- **Location:** 7 Soi Rambuttri, Chakrapong Road, Phra Nakhon
- **Price Range:** 800 – 1,500 THB per night ($22 – $42 USD).
- **Facilities:** Affordable guesthouse with private rooms, a small pool, and an on-site restaurant.
- **Nearby Attractions:** Walking distance to Khao San Road, the Grand Palace, and the Chao Phraya River.

BED STATION Hostel Ratchathewi

Why stay here?

Located just a short walk from the *Ratchathewi BTS Skytrain Station*, this hostel offers easy access to Bangkok's major attractions. Guests can enjoy modern amenities, including free Wi-Fi, air-conditioned rooms, and a communal lounge perfect for socializing. The hostel's industrial-chic design creates a cozy atmosphere, making it an ideal choice for solo travelers and groups alike. With its prime location and friendly environment, Bed Station Hostel Bangkok provides a memorable stay for those exploring the dynamic city.

- **Location:** 486/149-150 Petchaburi Road, Ratchathewi.
- **Price Range:** 500 – 1,000 THB per night ($14 – $28 USD).
- **Facilities:** Stylish hostel with shared and private rooms, a communal kitchen, and a bar.
- **Nearby Attractions:** Near BTS Ratchathewi, close to MBK Center and Siam Paragon.

Unique stays: Treehouses and Eco-Lodges

For travelers looking for an unusual experience, Bangkok offers unique eco-friendly stays that allow you to connect with nature or explore a different side of the city. Here are some of the top unique stays in Bangkok:

Bangkok Tree House

Why stay here?

The Bangkok Tree House is a hidden gem nestled along the peaceful banks of the Chao Phraya River, offering an eco-friendly escape from the city's bustling streets. This unique boutique hotel provides guests with treehouse-style rooms elevated among the mangroves, giving a feeling of being immersed in nature while still near Bangkok's dynamic center. With rooftop decks, open-air showers, and sustainable practices, including solar power and recycling, the Bangkok Tree House offers a tranquil, eco-conscious experience where you can truly reconnect with nature. It's an ideal spot for travelers looking to experience Bangkok's greener, quieter side.

- **Location:** 60 Moo 1, Bang Nam Phueng, Phra Pradaeng District.
- **Price Range:** 3,000 – 5,000 THB per night ($85 – $140 USD).
- **Facilities:** A hidden gem located along the Chao Phraya River, Bangkok Tree House offers.
- **Nearby Attractions:** Close to Bang Krachao, Bangkok's "Green Lung" and a popular cycling spot.

Green Leaf Hostel

Why stay here?

Green Leaf Hostel Bangkok is an eco-friendly haven nestled in the heart of Bangkok. Perfect for budget travelers and eco-conscious guests, this hostel combines comfort with sustainable practices, offering clean, minimalist rooms and dorms at affordable rates. With its green initiatives, including recycling programs and energy-efficient designs, Green Leaf provides a refreshing, guilt-free stay. Located close to Bangkok's bustling markets and iconic attractions, it's an ideal base for exploring the city's rich culture while connecting with like-minded travelers in a welcoming atmosphere.

- **Location:** 40/10 Sukhumvit 89, Bang Chak.
- **Price Range:** 1,000 – 2,500 THB per night ($28 – $70 USD).
- **Facilities:** Features a bamboo décor, recycling initiatives, and green spaces. Additionally, private rooms and dorms offer a serene, budget-friendly stay with a focus on sustainability.
- **Nearby Attractions:** Accessible to BTS Bang Chak, close to local markets and cafes.

iSanook Bangkok

Why stay here?

The iSanook Bangkok is a modern hotel located in the heart of Bangkok, blending comfort with style for travelers seeking an affordable yet unique stay. Known for its contemporary design and warm hospitality, iSanook offers cozy rooms, a rooftop pool with city views, and a relaxed atmosphere that appeals to both tourists and business travelers. With easy access to popular sites like the Grand Palace and bustling markets, it's an ideal base for exploring Bangkok's rich culture.

- **Location:** 118 Soi Songphra, Siphraya Road, Maha Phruttharam, Bang Rak.
- **Price Range:** 1,200 – 3,000 THB per night ($35 – $85 USD)
- **Facilities:** Offers studio apartments with communal areas, a rooftop garden, and a small pool. The hotel emphasizes responsible tourism, making it a great choice for eco-conscious travelers.
- **Nearby Attractions:** Close to Chinatown, the Chao Phraya River, and MRT Sam Yan station.

CHAPTER SIX

Bangkok's Must-See Attractions

Bangkok is a city of contrasts, where rich history meets dynamic modernity, and cultural landmarks exist alongside bustling urban life. From breathtaking temples to serene parks, here are Bangkok's must-see attractions that capture the spirit and culture of Thailand's capital.

Historical Landmarks and Temples

Bangkok's temples and historical landmarks reflect the city's deep-rooted spiritual and cultural heritage. Each site offers a unique insight into Thailand's past, with stunning architecture and fascinating histories that make them unmissable.

The Grand Palace and Wat Phra Kaew

The Grand Palace is Bangkok's most iconic attraction, a sprawling complex that has served as the official residence of Thailand's kings since 1782. With its grand architecture, gold-plated structures, and intricate details, it remains a symbol of Thailand's royal heritage.

Wat Phra Kaew

Within the Grand Palace grounds is Wat Phra Kaew, known as The Temple of the Emerald Buddha, Thailand's most sacred temple. It houses the revered Emerald Buddha, carved from a single jade stone, and is surrounded by breathtaking murals depicting tales from Buddhist mythology. The intricate artistry, dynamic murals, and detailed statues make Wat Phra Kaew a remarkable place of worship and cultural preservation.

- **Location:** Na Phra Lan Road, Phra Nakhon District, near the Chao Phraya River.
- **Entry Fee and Opening Hours:** Entry fees are around 500 THB ($14), and it's open daily from 8:30 AM to 3:30 PM.
- **Visiting Tip:** Visitors must dress modestly, covering shoulders and knees.

Wat Arun (Temple of Dawn)

Known for its stunning riverside location and unique design, Wat Arun is one of Bangkok's most recognizable temples. Standing at over 70 meters tall, the temple's main pagoda (prang) is covered in colorful porcelain and ceramic tiles, reflecting the sun and creating a radiant display, especially at sunrise and sunset. The temple's name, *Wat Arun*, translates to "Temple of Dawn", and it's a beautiful sight at any time of day.

- **Location:** Arun Amarin Road.
- **Entry Fee and Opening Hours:** Entry fees are 100 THB ($3), and it's open from 8:00 AM to 5:30 PM.
- **Visiting Tip:** A quick ferry ride across the river from Wat Pho makes it easy to visit both temples in one trip.

Wat Pho (The Temple of the Reclining Buddha)

Wat Pho is famous for its massive reclining Buddha, which stretches 46 meters long and is covered in gold leaf. The temple is one of the oldest in Bangkok, dating back to the 16th century, and is considered a significant center for traditional Thai massage. Wat Pho is also home to Thailand's oldest public education center, with murals, inscriptions, and statues that illustrate various subjects.

- **Location:** 2 Sanamchai Road, close to the Grand Palace and Wat Arun.
- **Entry Fee and Opening Hours:** Entry fees are around 200 THB ($5.50), and the temple is open daily from 8:00 AM to 6:30 PM.
- **Visiting Tip:** After exploring the temple, try a traditional Thai massage at the temple's renowned massage school for a unique experience.

Museums and Galleries

For those interested in art, history, and culture, Bangkok's museums and galleries offer a mix of traditional and contemporary exhibitions that delve into Thailand's diverse heritage.

Bangkok National Museum

As Thailand's largest museum, the Bangkok National Museum houses an extensive collection of Thai art and artifacts, including sculptures, textiles, ceramics, and weapons. The museum provides a comprehensive overview of Thailand's history and culture, from ancient times to modern-day.

- **Location:** Na Phra That Road, Phra Nakhon District, near the Grand Palace.
- **Entry Fee and Opening Hours:** Entry fee is 200 THB ($5.50), and it's open Wednesday to Sunday from 9:00 AM to 4:00 PM.
- **Visiting Tip:** Guided tours are available in English, providing valuable insights into the museum's exhibits and Thailand's history.

Jim Thompson House and Museum

Once home to the American businessman and Thai silk entrepreneur *Jim Thompson,* this beautifully preserved traditional Thai house offers an intimate look into traditional Thai architecture and art. The museum displays Thompson's personal collection of Asian art and artifacts, and the lush garden surroundings create a peaceful atmosphere.

- **Location:** 6 Soi Kasemsan 2, Rama I Road, near BTS National Stadium Station.
- **Entry Fee and Opening Hours:** Tickets are available at 200 THB ($5.50), and it opens daily from 9:00 AM to 6:00 PM.
- **Visiting Tip:** Guided tours are included in the entry fee, allowing visitors to learn about Thompson's life and his contributions to Thai culture.

Museum of Contemporary Art (MOCA)

MOCA is a premier destination for contemporary art lovers, showcasing an impressive collection of Thai and international modern art, and a vast collection of Thai contemporary art that showcases Thailand's creative evolution. The museum's five floors include sculptures, paintings, and mixed media pieces that reflect Thai culture, Buddhism, and modern influences.

- **Location:** 499 Vibhavadi Rangsit Road, Chatuchak District.
- **Entry Fee and Opening Hours:** Admission is 250 THB ($7), and it's open from Tuesday to Sunday, 10:00 AM to 6:00 PM.
- **Visiting Tip:** MOCA is slightly off the beaten path, so taking a taxi or ride-share from the nearest BTS station (Mo Chit) is recommended.

Museum of Siam

The Museum of Siam presents Thailand's history with a modern twist, using interactive exhibits to engage visitors in a unique exploration of Thai identity and culture. Each exhibit is designed to be fun and educational, making it a great choice for families and those interested in an immersive experience.

- **Location**: Sanam Chai Road, near Wat Pho.

- **Entry Fee and Opening Hours:** : Admission is 100 THB ($3) for adults, and it's open from Tuesday to Sunday, 10:00 AM to 6:00 PM.

Parks and Outdoor Spaces

Bangkok may be known for its bustling city life, but it's also home to several green spaces where visitors can relax, exercise, and enjoy a quieter side of the city. Below are some of the top parks and outdoor spaces in Bangkok:

Lumphini Park

Lumphini Park is Bangkok's largest and most popular park, offering a peaceful escape from the city's hustle and bustle. With its lakes, jogging paths, outdoor gym, and paddleboat rentals, the park is ideal for morning jogs, picnics, or simply unwinding in a natural setting. The park is also home to monitor lizards, which can be spotted around the lake.

- **Location:** Rama IV Road, near Silom and Ratchadamri areas.
- **Entry Fee:** Free.
- **Visiting Tip:** Visit in the early morning or late afternoon when temperatures are cooler, and join the locals in tai chi or aerobics classes.

Benjakitti Park

Benjakitti Park is known for its large lake surrounded by walking and cycling paths, offering a beautiful view of Bangkok's skyline. The park is especially scenic at sunset, with a boardwalk and new green spaces recently added to make it a favorite for both locals and tourists.

- **Location:** Ratchadaphisek Road, near BTS Asok Station.
- **Entry Fee:** Free.
- **Visiting Tip:** Bikes are available to rent, making it a perfect spot for cycling enthusiasts who want to explore the park's trails.

Chatuchak Park

Located next to the famous *Chatuchak Weekend Market,* Chatuchak Park is a serene green space with shaded walking paths, ponds, and picnic areas. It's a perfect place to relax after a day of shopping, with many locals and visitors taking advantage of the park's peaceful setting.

- **Location:** Kamphaeng Phet Road, near BTS Mo Chit Station.
- **Entry Fee:** Free.
- **Visiting Tip:** If visiting on a weekend, combine your trip with a visit to the Chatuchak Market for a complete Bangkok experience.

Bang Krachao (Bangkok's Green Lung)

Known as Bangkok's "Green Lung," Bang Krachao is a lush, forested area that feels worlds away from the city's bustling streets. The area is ideal for cycling, with bike rentals available for exploring its quiet roads, mangroves, and small farms. Bang Krachao also hosts a floating market on weekends, offering local produce and street food.

- **Location:** Across the Chao Phraya River, reachable by boat from Klong Toei Pier.
- **Entry Fee:** Free (small boat fare to cross the river).
- **Visiting Tip:** Rent a bike to fully explore this natural oasis and escape the urban intensity of Bangkok.

Santichaiprakarn Park

Located along the Chao Phraya River, Santichaiprakarn Park is known for its historic Phra Sumen Fort and riverfront views. The park is a relaxing spot to watch the sunset over the river or enjoy the view of passing boats.

- **Location**: Phra Athit Road, close to Khao San Road.
- **Entry Fee:** Free.
- **Visiting Tip**: It's a popular place for picnics and evening strolls, particularly with views of the Rama VIII Bridge.

King Rama IX Park

King Rama IX Park is Bangkok's largest green space, offering beautiful gardens, lakes, and a botanical garden. Created in honor of King Bhumibol's 60th birthday, the park includes themed gardens, water features, and plenty of walking trails, ideal for nature lovers.

- **Location**: Suan Luang District, about a 20-minute drive from downtown.
- **Entry Fee:** Entry is 10 THB ($0.30).
- **Visiting Tip:** Early mornings are best to experience the park's peaceful ambiance.

Bangkok's must-see attractions offer a diverse experience, blending history, art, and natural beauty. Whether you're exploring sacred temples, delving into the city's rich history at a museum, or relaxing in a riverside park, Bangkok provides countless opportunities to immerse yourself in the city's unique culture and charm. Each of these attractions highlights a different facet of Bangkok, making your journey through the city truly unforgettable.

CHAPTER SEVEN

Cultural Insights and Local Experiences

Bangkok is a city deeply rooted in cultural traditions and social etiquette, with customs shaped by Thailand's predominant religion, Buddhism, and its unique heritage. Understanding these cultural aspects can greatly enhance your travel experience, offering insights into the ways Thai people express respect, celebrate, and connect with each other. Here's what you need to know about Thai customs, Buddhism, major festivals, and key phrases to help you navigate Bangkok with cultural sensitivity and respect:

Thai Customs and Social Etiquettes

Respect and politeness are cornerstones of Thai culture, and understanding a few key customs can help you navigate social interactions respectfully. The following are key criterias in Thai customs and social etiquettes:

- **The Wai Greeting:** The "wai" is a traditional Thai greeting where hands are placed together in a prayer-like position, and the head is slightly bowed. It's a sign of respect, with the height of the hands indicating the degree of respect (higher for elders or monks). While locals don't expect foreigners to perform the wai, a slight bow or smile is appreciated in response.

- **Respect for the Monarchy**: The Thai monarchy is highly revered, and respect for the king and royal family is deeply ingrained in Thai culture. It's common to see portraits of the king in public spaces, and criticizing the monarchy is against the law. When the national anthem plays (typically at 8:00 AM and 6:00 PM in public places), locals stop and stand in respect, and visitors are expected to do the same.

- **Respect for Elders and Hierarchies:** Thai society places great importance on age and status, so respect for elders and authority figures is essential. Use polite language and show deference to those older than you, especially in formal or traditional settings.

- **Head and Feet Etiquette:** In Thai culture, the head is considered the most sacred part of the body, while feet are the lowest. Avoid touching anyone's head, and never point your feet at people or religious statues. When sitting, especially in temples, try to sit cross-legged or with feet tucked behind you.

- **Dress Modestly at Temples:** Temples are sacred places, and dressing appropriately is crucial. Wear clothing that covers shoulders and knees, and avoid sleeveless tops or shorts. Shoes are usually removed before entering the main temple buildings.

- **Saving Face**: The Thai people have a strong cultural concept of "saving face", which involves avoiding embarrassment or confrontation. Raising your voice, displaying anger, or causing someone to lose face is considered very rude. It's best to approach situations with a calm and polite attitude.

Understanding Religion: Buddhism in Bangkok

Approximately 95% of the Thai people are Buddhist, and Buddhism plays a central role in Thai culture. Bangkok, as Thailand's capital, is home to hundreds of temples, each a testament to the country's deep spiritual roots.

- **The Role of Buddhism:** Buddhism in Thailand follows the Theravada tradition, emphasizing meditation, karma, and the pursuit of enlightenment. Monks are respected figures in society, and it's common to see locals offering alms (donations) to monks, especially in the mornings. Many Thai people visit temples regularly to make merit, pray, and seek blessings.

- **Temple Etiquette:** When visiting temples, show respect by dressing modestly, keeping voices low, and avoiding inappropriate gestures. Photography restricted in certain areas, so look for signs or ask if unsure. If you wish to make a small donation, there are usually collection boxes where offerings can be placed.

- **Respecting Monks:** Monks are highly regarded, and certain customs are observed in their presence. For example, women should avoid touching monks or handing items directly to them; instead, place the item nearby or pass it through a male intermediary. When seated near monks, try to sit lower or at a respectful distance.

- **Spirit Houses:** Spirit houses are small, decorative shrines found outside homes, businesses, and public spaces. Thais believe they provide shelter for protective spirits, and they are often adorned with offerings of flowers, food, and incense. Admire them from a distance, but avoid touching them as a sign of respect.

Festivals and Events: Songkran, Loi Krathong, and More

Bangkok hosts several dynamic festivals throughout the year, each with unique customs, rituals, and opportunities to connect with Thai culture. The following are some of the main festivals and events held in Bangkok:

Songkran (Thai New Year)

Songkran is one of Thailand's most famous festivals, marking the traditional Thai New Year with water-based celebrations. Originally, people sprinkled water to wash away bad luck, but it has evolved into a nationwide water fight. In Bangkok, entire streets turn into water-soaked playgrounds where locals and visitors douse each other with water guns and buckets. It's a time of joy and unity, and participants are encouraged to bring waterproof gear and join the fun. Be prepared to get wet, and keep valuables in waterproof bags!

- **Date:** April 13–15.

- **Location:** Celebrated throughout Bangkok, with major events in areas like Silom, Khao San Road, and Phra Pradaeng.

Loi Krathong (Festival of Lights)

Loi Krathong is a beautiful festival where people float decorated baskets (krathongs) made of banana leaves, flowers, and candles on water as an offering to the river goddess. The act of releasing the krathong is believed to symbolize letting go of past misfortunes. Bangkok's rivers and lakes are illuminated with thousands of floating lights, creating a serene and magical atmosphere.

- **Date:** November, on the evening of the full moon in the 12th lunar month.
- **Location:** Most popular locations include Chao Phraya River, Wat Saket (Golden Mount), Asiatique, and Lumphini Park.

King's Birthday and Father's Day

December 5th is a national holiday that commemorates the birthday of the late *King Bhumibol Adulyadej*, who is remembered with great reverence. The day is also celebrated as Father's Day in Thailand. The city is decorated with lights and royal symbols, with grand ceremonies and floral displays, particularly along Ratchadamnoen Avenue.

- **Date:** December 5th.
- **Location:** Grand Palace, Ratchadamnoen Avenue, and across the city.

Chinese New Year

The Chinese New Year is celebrated with enthusiasm in Bangkok's Chinatown, where processions, dragon dances, and street food stalls create a lively scene. Locals and tourists flock to *Yaowarat* to enjoy the festive decorations, fireworks, and delicious Chinese delicacies.

- **Date:** January or February, depending on the lunar calendar.
- **Location:** Yaowarat Road, Bangkok's Chinatown.

Makha Bucha Day

Makha Bucha Day commemorates the Buddha's teachings and is a significant Buddhist holiday in Thailand. Devotees visit temples to make merit and participate in candlelit processions. It's a quieter, more solemn festival, giving visitors a chance to observe Thai religious practices in a respectful, reflective setting.

- **Date:** Varies, depending on the lunar calendar (usually February).
- **Location:** Temples across Bangkok, including Wat Pho and Wat Arun.

Language Basics and Key Thai Phrases

While English is widely spoken in tourist areas, learning a few basic Thai phrases can go a long way in showing respect and building rapport with locals. Thai is a tonal language, so pronunciation can change the meaning of a word, but don't worry—the Thai people appreciate the effort!

Greetings and Courtesies:

- **Hello:** *Sawasdee* (สวัสดี).

Add *khrub* (for males) or *ka* (for females) at the end for politeness. E.g., *Sawasdee khrub* ("Hello" for a man) or *Sawasdee ka* ("Hello" for a woman).

- **Thank You:** *Khob khun* (ขอบคุณ).

Similar to greetings, add *khrub* or *ka* for extra politeness: *Khob khun khrub/ka.*

- **Excuse me/Sorry:** *Kho tot* (ขอโทษ).

Basic Questions:

- **How much?** - *Tao rai?* (เท่าไหร่).

- **Where is…?** - *Yoo tee nai?* (อยู่ที่ไหน).
- **Can you help me?** - *Chuey dai mai?*

Helpful Words:

- **Yes:** *Chai* (ใช่).
- **No:** *Mai chai* (ไม่ใช่).
- **Delicious:** *Aroi* (อร่อย).
- **I don't understand:** *Mai kao jai* (ไม่เข้าใจ).

Polite Responses:

Adding *khrub* (ครับ) or *ka* (ค่ะ) at the end of sentences is a simple way to show respect. Even if you don't master Thai, ending phrases with *khrub* or *ka* is appreciated and polite.

Making the effort to speak even a little Thai often brings a smile from locals and creates a more positive interaction. Remember, Thai people value politeness and friendliness, so a warm attitude goes a long way.

CHAPTER EIGHT

Dining in Bangkok

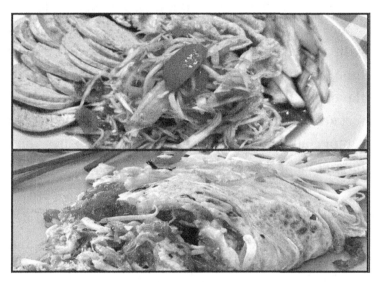

Bangkok is a paradise for food lovers, with a culinary scene as dynamic and diverse as the city itself. From the sizzling sounds of street food vendors to the fine dining establishments of world-renowned chefs, Bangkok offers endless food experiences to satisfy every craving. Here's a guide to the best dining experiences, traditional dishes, and food markets to make your journey through Bangkok's flavors unforgettable.

Bangkok's Culinary Scene

Bangkok's culinary landscape reflects a fusion of flavors influenced by Thai, Chinese, Indian, and Western cuisines. Known for its balance of spicy, sour, sweet, and salty flavors, Thai food is packed with ingredients like lemongrass, chili, garlic, and lime, creating dishes that are both aromatic and flavorful. From street food vendors to upscale restaurants, the city provides countless ways to sample authentic Thai cuisine, fusion dishes, and international flavors.

Traditional Street Food Must-Try Dishes

Bangkok's street food scene is legendary, and sampling from street vendors is a must for any visitor. Here are some classic Thai dishes to try:

Pad Thai

This iconic stir-fried noodle dish combines rice noodles with shrimp or chicken, tofu, eggs, bean sprouts, and peanuts, topped with lime and chili for added flavor. Pad Thai is a perfect balance of flavors and is available from street vendors across the city.

- **Average Price Range:** 40–80 THB ($1.10–$2.20).

Som Tum (Papaya Salad)

A spicy and refreshing salad made from shredded green papaya, peanuts, tomatoes, chilies, and lime juice. It's both spicy and tangy, offering a refreshing break from heavier dishes. Som Tum can be found at street stalls and food markets like Chatuchak.

- **Average Price Range:** 30–60 THB ($0.85–$1.70).

Tom Yum Goong (Spicy Shrimp Soup)

A fragrant soup with shrimp, lemongrass, kaffir lime leaves, galangal, and chilies, creating a bold, spicy, and sour flavor. Tom Yum is often found in local eateries and street markets.

- **Average Price Range:** 50–100 THB ($1.40–$2.80).

Mango Sticky Rice

This dish is a well-known dessert made with sweet sticky rice, ripe mango and coconut milk. It's tasty, creamy, and the best way to finish a meal. You'll find mango sticky rice at many food stalls and markets.

- **Average Price Range:** 50–80 THB ($1.40–$2.20).

Khao Man Gai (Chicken Rice)

This simple yet flavorful dish features tender poached chicken served over rice cooked in chicken broth, accompanied by a garlic-ginger sauce. It's commonly available at food stalls across Bangkok.

- **Average Price:** 30–50 THB ($0.85–$1.40).

Top Restaurants: Fine Dining

For travelers looking to enjoy fine dining, Bangkok offers some incredible restaurants where Thai cuisine is elevated to an art form. Here are five top spots:

Gaggan Anand, Bangkok

Why dine here?

Gaggan Anand is a dining experience like no other, led by the visionary *chef Gaggan Anand*, known for redefining Indian cuisine. Located in Bangkok, this Michelin-starred restaurant takes guests on a bold, playful journey through Indian flavors with a modern twist, blending artistry and creativity in every dish. The tasting menu, often served with an air of mystery, surprises diners with unexpected textures, presentations, and flavors that challenge the boundaries of traditional Indian food. At Gaggan Anand, dining becomes an immersive adventure—one where every course is designed to evoke emotions and tell a story, making it a must-visit for food enthusiasts worldwide.

- **Location:** Soi Sukhumvit 31, Khlong Tan Nuea.
- **Price Range**: 6,500–9,000 THB ($180–$250) for tasting menus.
- **Cuisine:** Progressive Indian menus with Thai influences.

Le Du, Bangkok

Why dine here?

Le Du in Bangkok is a celebrated culinary gem that brings modern Thai flavors to life with innovative twists. Founded by Chef Thitid "Ton" Tassanakajohn, a Le Cordon Bleu-trained chef, Le Du takes diners on a seasonal journey through Thailand's diverse ingredients. The restaurant's name, derived from the Thai word for "season", reflects its dedication to using fresh, local produce to craft creative dishes that honor traditional Thai flavors while embracing contemporary techniques.

Located in the dynamic Silom district, Le Du's tasting menu offers a bold, refined take on Thai cuisine, making it a must-visit for food enthusiasts seeking an unforgettable dining experience in Bangkok.

- **Location:** Silom Soi 7, Silom.
- **Price Range:** 3,500–4,500 THB ($100–$130) for tasting menus.
- **Cuisine:** Modern Thai cuisine.

Nahm, Bangkok

Why dine here?

Nahm is a renowned culinary gem that brings authentic Thai flavors to life in a contemporary, refined setting. Located in Bangkok's Sathorn district, Nahm is celebrated for its innovative yet deeply traditional dishes crafted by skilled chefs who honor Thailand's culinary heritage. With a menu that draws from age-old recipes and local ingredients, dining at Nahm is a journey through Thailand's rich gastronomic landscape. The restaurant's warm ambiance, combined with its attention to detail and artistry, makes it a must-visit for anyone seeking an elevated Thai dining experience in Bangkok

- **Location:** COMO Metropolitan Bangkok, Sathorn.
- **Price Range:** 2,500–4,500 THB ($70–$130) for tasting menus.
- **Cuisine:** Authentic Thai cuisine.

Sorn, Bangkok

Why dine here?

Sorn is a renowned Thai fine-dining restaurant celebrated for its authentic Southern Thai cuisine and immersive dining experience. Located in Sukhumvit, Sorn takes guests on a flavorful journey through Thailand's southern provinces, emphasizing bold, aromatic ingredients and traditional cooking methods. Founded by Chef Supaksorn "Ice" Jongsiri, Sorn has earned a Michelin star and global recognition for its commitment to seasonal, local produce and seafood. Each dish is crafted to reflect the rich cultural heritage of Southern Thailand, making Sorn a must-visit for food enthusiasts seeking an unforgettable taste of Thai culinary artistry.

- **Location:** Sukhumvit Soi 26, Khlong Tan Nuea.
- **Price Range:** 3,200–4,800 THB ($90–$140) for tasting menus.
- **Cuisine:** Southern Thai cuisine.

Paste, Bangkok

Why dine here?

Paste is a Michelin-starred restaurant celebrated for its innovative take on traditional Thai cuisine. Located in the heart of Bangkok, Paste combines dynamic flavors with an artistic presentation, offering a modern twist on age-old Thai recipes inspired by royal and regional influences. Chef Bee Satongun, a master of Thai flavors, creates dishes that highlight seasonal ingredients and rare herbs, creating a unique sensory experience that honors Thailand's rich culinary heritage. With its sophisticated ambiance and bold, authentic flavors, Paste is a must-visit for those seeking an elevated Thai dining experience in Bangkok.

- **Location:** Gaysorn Village Mall, Ratchaprasong.
- **Price Range:** 2,500–4,500 THB ($70–$130) for tasting menus.
- **Cuisine:** Thai Fusion cuisine.

Budget-Friendly Restaurants in Bangkok

For travelers looking for affordable yet delicious options, Bangkok has a wealth of budget-friendly eateries that serve amazing dishes without breaking the bank. Here are five popular spots:

P'Aor Tom Yum Goong Noodles, Bangkok

Why dine here?

This restaurant is a hidden gem in Bangkok that's famous for serving some of the city's best *Tom Yum Goong* (spicy prawn soup) noodles. Nestled in the bustling streets of the Phaya Thai district, this humble eatery attracts locals and tourists alike with its richly flavored, creamy Tom Yum broth, which balances spicy, sour, and savory notes to perfection. The dish features generous portions of fresh prawns, squid, and thick noodles that absorb the aromatic broth, creating a meal that's as satisfying as it is flavorful. Known for its authentic taste and affordable prices, P'Aor is a must-visit spot for anyone seeking a true taste of Bangkok's dynamic street food scene.

- **Location:** Soi Petchaburi 5, Ratchathewi.
- **Price Range:** 50–200 THB ($1.40–$5.50).
- **Cuisine:** Thai Seafood.

Thipsamai Pad Thai, Bangkok

Why dine here?

Thipsamai Pad Thai in Bangkok is a legendary spot for authentic Pad Thai, often hailed as one of the best in Thailand. Established in 1966, this iconic eatery serves its famous Pad Thai wrapped in a delicate layer of egg, cooked over a charcoal fire for a unique smoky flavor. Located in Bangkok's Old Town, Thipsamai often has lines of locals and tourists eager to try its flavorful, perfectly balanced dishes. The "Superb Pad Thai" is a must-try, featuring fresh prawns, bean sprouts, and tamarind sauce, making it an unforgettable taste of Bangkok's culinary heritage.

- **Location:** Maha Chai Road, near Wat Saket.
- **Price Range:** 70–100 THB ($2–$3).
- **Cuisine:** Thai cuisine.

Krua Apsorn, Bangkok

Why dine here?

Krua Apsorn in Bangkok is a beloved spot for authentic Thai cuisine, known for its classic flavors and royal-inspired recipes. This restaurant has earned a stellar reputation among locals and tourists alike for its expertly crafted dishes, like *crab omelets, green curry,* and *stir-fried lotus stems with shrimp.* Simple and unpretentious in ambiance, *Krua Apsorn* lets the food shine, making it a must-visit for anyone looking to experience traditional Thai flavors in a truly local setting. Don't miss their signature yellow curry with prawns—an unforgettable taste of Bangkok.

- **Location:** Dinso Road, near Democracy Monument.
- **Price Range:** 100–300 THB ($3–$8).
- **Cuisine:** Traditional Thai cuisine.

Jay Fai, Bangkok

Why dine here?

Jay Fai, a legendary street food spot in Bangkok, is famous worldwide for its flavorful dishes and iconic chef, Supinya Junsuta, known as "Jay Fai". With her trademark ski goggles and fiery wok, Jay Fai crafts sensational dishes like *crab omelets* and d*runken noodles* that have earned her a Michelin star and devoted customers. Located in the bustling streets of Bangkok's Old Town, this humble eatery blends high-quality ingredients with traditional Thai flavors, creating a dining experience that's both authentic and unforgettable. Be prepared for long waits, as food lovers from all over the world line up to taste her renowned creations!

- **Location:** Mahachai Road, near Samran Rat Intersection.
- **Price Range:** 400–1,000 THB ($11–$28).
- **Cuisine:** Thai Street Food.

Somsak Pu Ob, Bangkok

Somsak Pu Ob is a must-visit gem in Bangkok for seafood lovers, famous for its delicious P*u Ob Woon Sen*—a flavorful dish of fresh crab and glass noodles cooked in a clay pot. Tucked away in a humble, open-air stall, Somsak Pu Ob attracts locals and tourists alike for its simple, authentic setup and unforgettable flavors. The noodles absorb a rich blend of soy sauce, garlic, ginger, and spices, while the crab is tender and sweet. Arrive early, as lines can get long, but the taste is well worth the wait!

- **Location**: Soi Charoen Rat 1, Thonburi.
- **Price Range:** 150–300 THB ($4–$8).
- **Cuisine**: Thai Seafood.

Markets for Food Lovers

Bangkok's food markets are the heart of the city's culinary culture. These bustling venues offer an array of fresh produce, street food, and local delicacies. Here are three of the best markets for food enthusiasts:

Chatuchak Weekend Market

Why dine here?

Chatuchak is one of the world's largest markets, with over 15,000 stalls selling everything from clothing to food. Food lovers can sample a range of street food, including grilled meat skewers, coconut ice cream, and mango sticky rice.

- **Location:** Kamphaeng Phet Road, near BTS Mo Chit.
- **Day and Time:** Open Saturdays and Sundays, 9:00 AM–6:00 PM
- **Must-Try:** Coconut ice cream, grilled meat skewers, fried quail eggs.
- **Visiting Tips:** Go early to avoid the crowds and bring cash, as most vendors don't accept cards.

Yaowarat (Chinatown)

Why dine here?

Chinatown is a bustling night market known for its diverse array of street food, from Chinese-style buns to traditional Thai desserts. It's a great place to try dishes like dumplings, seafood, and noodle soups, with many vendors open late into the night.

- **Location:** Yaowarat Road, accessible by MRT Wat Mangkon.
- **Time:** Most active in the evenings.
- **Must-Try:** Crispy pork, dim sum, herbal teas.
- **Visiting Tips:** Bring an appetite and explore different stalls to sample a variety of flavors.

Or Tor Kor Market

Why dine here?

Or Tor Kor Market in Bangkok is a must-visit for food enthusiasts, known for its premium-quality produce, fresh seafood, and exotic Thai ingredients. Unlike typical street markets, Or Tor Kor offers an upscale market experience, showcasing a dynamic selection of tropical fruits, spices, and ready-to-eat Thai delicacies. Located near the famous *Chatuchak Market*, it's an ideal stop for sampling authentic Thai flavors and grabbing unique food souvenirs in a clean and well-organized setting.

- **Location:** Kamphaeng Phet Road, across from Chatuchak Market.
- **Day and Time:** Opens daily from 6:00 AM to 8:00 PM..
- **Must-Try:** Tropical fruits, Thai sweets, and fresh seafood.
- **Visiting Tips:** This market is perfect for foodies who want to explore local

ingredients, as this market has the best selection of fruits and regional products.

Bangkok's dining and food experiences offer something for everyone, from adventurous street food to high-end culinary creations. With this guide, you're set to savor the best flavors the city has to offer, making your Bangkok visit a journey through Thailand's delicious and diverse cuisine.

CHAPTER NINE

Nightlife and Entertainment in Bangkok

Bangkok's nightlife is dynamic, diverse, and offers something for everyone. From sophisticated rooftop lounges and trendy bars to lively nightclubs, traditional performances, and thrilling Muay Thai matches, the city's after-dark scene is as colorful as it is exciting. Here's your guide to the best nightlife spots in Bangkok to make your evenings as memorable as your days.

Best Bars and Rooftop Lounges

Bangkok is famous for its rooftop bars that offer stunning views of the city skyline and the Chao Phraya River. These lounges are perfect for sipping a cocktail as the sun sets or admiring the city's glittering lights at night.

Sky Bar at Lebua State Tower

As one of the world's highest open-air bars, Sky Bar offers jaw-dropping views from the 63rd floor of the Lebua State Tower. Known for its golden dome and signature cocktails, including the iconic

Hangovertini, Sky Bar attracts both tourists and locals seeking a glamorous night out.

- **Location:** 63rd Floor, 1055 Silom Road, Bang Rak.
- **Visiting Tip:** There's a smart casual dress code, so avoid flip-flops and shorts.

Vertigo and Moon Bar at Banyan Tree

Vertigo offers a fine dining experience with a spectacular view, while Moon Bar serves up an impressive selection of cocktails. Perched atop the

Banyan Tree Hotel, this bar offers 360-degree views of Bangkok's cityscape and is especially romantic at sunset.

- **Location:** 61st Floor, 21/100 South Sathon Road, Sathon.
- **Visiting Tip:** Reservations are recommended, especially during peak hours.

Octave Rooftop Lounge & Bar

Octave is a multi-level rooftop bar offering panoramic views and a lively ambiance. Known for its trendy vibe and creative cocktails, Octave is a favorite spot for socializing with a young and energetic crowd.

- **Location:** 45th Floor, Marriott Hotel Sukhumvit, 2 Sukhumvit Soi 57.
- **Visiting Tip:** The bar has three levels, each offering a different atmosphere, so explore to find your preferred spot.

Above Eleven, Bangkok

This rooftop bar blends Bangkok's skyline with a taste of Peruvian-Japanese cuisine. Above Eleven's unique setting and delicious cocktails make it an ideal place for a relaxed yet stylish night out.

- **Location:** 33rd Floor, Fraser Suites Sukhumvit, 38/8 Sukhumvit Soi 11.
- **Visiting Tip:** Try their famous Pisco Sour for a touch of Peru in Bangkok.

Maggie Choo's, Bangkok

Maggie Choo's is a speakeasy-style bar with 1930s Shanghai-inspired décor. Known for its live jazz performances, plush velvet seating, and dimly lit ambiance, it offers a unique blend of old-world charm and contemporary vibes.

- **Location:** Basement of Novotel Bangkok Fenix Silom, 320 Silom Road, Bang Rak.
- **Visiting Tip:** Arrive early for live music and enjoy the sultry atmosphere before the bar fills up.

Nightclubs and Live Music Venues

Bangkok's nightclubs and live music venues offer everything from electronic beats to jazz performances, making it easy to find a spot that suits your taste.

Levels Club & Lounge

With a spacious dance floor, private lounges, and multiple rooms playing different music genres,

Levels is popular for its lively atmosphere and international DJs. It's a great spot for partygoers looking to dance the night away.

- **Location:** 6th Floor, Aloft Bangkok Hotel, 35 Sukhumvit Soi 11.
- **Visiting Tip:** Dress to impress, as the club has a smart casual dress code.

Route 66 Club, Bangkok

Route 66 is one of Bangkok's most famous clubs, with different rooms offering hip-hop, electronic, and Thai pop music. Known for its high-energy vibe and large crowds, it's a local favorite.

- **Location:** RCA Plaza, Rama IX Road, Huai Khwang.
- **Visiting Tip:** Route 66 is cash only, so bring some Thai Baht for entry and drinks.

The Iron Fairies, Bangkok

A unique blend of art and live jazz, Iron Fairies is a fairy-tale-themed bar with wrought-iron details and quirky decor. This intimate venue offers jazz music in a whimsical setting, making it a great option for a quieter night with quality live performances.

- **Location:** 394 Sukhumvit Soi 55, Thonglor.
- **Visiting Tip:** Try their signature Iron Fairy burger, which pairs well with the live jazz atmosphere.

The Rock Pub, Bangkok

For rock music enthusiasts, *The Rock Pub* is a must-visit. With a cozy, unpretentious vibe, this long-standing pub features local and international rock bands playing everything from classic rock to heavy metal.

- **Location:** 93/26-28 Hollywood Street Building, Phaya Thai Road, near Ratchathewi BTS.
- **Visiting Tip:** Check their schedule online for specific band performances.

Sing Sing Theater

Combining theater with nightlife, *Sing Sing Theater* has an ornate design inspired by old Shanghai, complete with hanging lanterns and latticework. The club hosts themed nights, live DJs, and occasional performances, offering an unforgettable experience.

- **Location:** 37 Sukhumvit Soi 45, Khlong Tan Nuea.
- **Visiting Tip:** Arrive early, as it's a popular spot and can get crowded quickly.

Traditional Performances and Muay Thai

For a deeper connection with Thai culture, Bangkok offers traditional performances and Muay Thai matches, giving you a glimpse into the city's heritage.

Siam Niramit, Bangkok

Siam Niramit is a grand theater show that presents Thai culture, history, and folklore through music, dance, and stunning visual effects. With over 100 performers and intricate costumes, it's a captivating journey through Thailand's rich traditions.

- **Location:** 19 Tiamruammit Road, near Thailand Cultural Center MRT.
- **Tickets:** 1,500–2,000 THB ($42–$56).
- **Visiting Tip:** Arrive early to explore the traditional Thai village replica on-site before the show.

Aksra Theatre, Bangkok

Known for its traditional Thai puppet shows, Aksra Theatre offers an engaging experience where intricately crafted puppets bring Thai myths and folklore to life. Each puppet is controlled by multiple puppeteers, creating graceful, lifelike movements.

- **Location:** 3rd Floor, King Power Complex, Rangnam Road, near Victory Monument BTS.
- **Tickets:** Approximately 1,200 THB ($34).
- **Visiting Tip:** Shows are infrequent, so check the schedule and book tickets in advance.

Rajadamnern Stadium (Muay Thai)

For travelers seeking an authentic Muay Thai experience, Rajadamnern Stadium is the place to go. Established in 1945, it's one of Bangkok's oldest and most revered Muay Thai venues. Matches feature fighters from around the world and showcase the skill, strength, and cultural significance of Thailand's national sport.

- **Location:** Ratchadamnoen Nok Road, Phra Nakhon.
- **Tickets**: 1,000–2,000 THB ($28–$56) for ringside seats.
- **Visiting Tip**: The stadium holds matches several nights a week, and tickets can be purchased at the venue or online.

Bangkok's nightlife and entertainment scene are as diverse as the city itself, offering everything from sky-high cocktails to traditional performances and high-energy clubs. With this guide, you're ready to explore Bangkok's dynamic after-dark scene and enjoy the city's unique mix of modern and traditional entertainment options.

CHAPTER TEN

Shopping in Bangkok

Bangkok is a shopper's paradise, offering everything from luxury malls to bustling street markets and unique floating markets. The city's diverse shopping options make it easy to find everything from designer fashion to authentic Thai handicrafts. Whether you're looking for souvenirs, clothing, or local delicacies, here's a guide to the best places to shop, what to buy, and tips on navigating Bangkok's dynamic retail scene.

Top Malls and High-End Shopping

For travelers who enjoy modern, air-conditioned spaces with a variety of global and local brands, Bangkok's malls are perfect for a day of shopping. The following are some of the top malls in Bangkok:

Siam Paragon

Why shop here?

Siam Paragon is one of Bangkok's premier luxury malls, offering high-end brands like Chanel, Gucci, and Louis Vuitton. The mall also features an expansive gourmet supermarket, cinema complex, and the Sea Life Bangkok Ocean World aquarium, making it a popular choice for a full day of shopping and entertainment.

- **Location:** 991 Rama I Road, Pathum Wan District, near BTS Siam.
- **Visiting Tip:** Check out the Gourmet Market for international food products and Thai snacks to take home.

CentralWorld

Why shop here?

CentralWorld is one of the largest malls in Southeast Asia, featuring a mix of high-street and luxury brands, tech stores, and local boutiques. Its dynamic atmosphere is enhanced by food courts, restaurants, and entertainment options, including an ice-skating rink.

- **Location:** 999/9 Rama I Road, Pathum Wan District, near BTS Chit Lom and BTS Siam.
- **Visiting Tip**: Head to the 6th floor, where you'll find Thai designer brands and unique fashion pieces.

EmQuartier

Why shop here?

EmQuartier is a modern, upscale mall with luxury brands, trendy boutiques, and a fantastic selection of dining options. The mall's unique "Helix Quartier" spiral structure features restaurants overlooking a lush indoor garden, creating a stylish shopping experience.

- **Location:** 693 Sukhumvit Road, near BTS Phrom Phong.
- **Visiting Tip:** Visit the outdoor terrace for panoramic views of Bangkok's skyline.

Iconsiam

Why shop here?

Situated along the Chao Phraya River, Iconsiam offers a luxury shopping experience with both international and Thai brands. The mall is also home to SookSiam, a market-style area featuring regional Thai products, food, and crafts.

- **Location:** 299 Charoen Nakhon Road, Khlong San District, near BTS Gold Line Charoen Nakhon Station.
- **Visiting Tip:** Take the free Iconsiam shuttle boat from Sathorn Pier for a scenic arrival.

Terminal 21

Why shop here

Terminal 21 is known for its unique concept, where each floor represents a different global city, including Tokyo, London, and Istanbul. It features local boutiques, global brands, and themed decor, offering a fun shopping experience with affordable options.

- **Location:** 88 Sukhumvit Road, near BTS Asok and MRT Sukhumvit.
- **Visiting Tip:** Visit the lower levels for Thai fashion and accessories at reasonable prices.

Markets to Explore

Bangkok's markets are lively, colorful, and perfect for finding unique items. Here are some of the top markets to explore in Bangkok:

Chatuchak Weekend Market

Why shop here?

As previously discussed, *Chatuchak* is one of the largest markets in the world, with over 15,000 stalls selling everything from clothing and accessories to antiques and plants. The market is a must-visit for its eclectic selection and dynamic atmosphere.

- **Location:** Kamphaeng Phet Road, near BTS Mo Chit and MRT Chatuchak Park.
- **Visiting Tip:** Arrive early to avoid crowds, and bring cash, as many vendors don't accept cards.

Asiatique the Riverfront

Why shop here?

Asiatique combines a night market with a riverside shopping mall, offering boutique shops, restaurants, and entertainment like the Asiatique Sky Ferris wheel. It's a great spot for souvenir shopping in the evening, with plenty of options for food and entertainment.

- **Location:** Charoen Krung Road, near BTS Saphan Taksin and free shuttle boat from Sathorn Pier.
- **Visiting Tip:** Visit around sunset for views over the river and a pleasant evening ambiance.

Damnoen Saduak Floating Market

Why shop here?

This iconic floating market offers a glimpse into traditional Thai commerce, with vendors selling fruits, vegetables, and snacks from boats. It's popular among tourists for its unique experience and photo opportunities.

- **Location:** Damnoen Saduak District, Ratchaburi Province, about 1.5 hours from Bangkok.
- **Visiting Tip:** Go early in the morning to see the market in full swing, and consider booking a guided tour for convenience.

Talad Rot Fai (Train Market)

Why shop here?

Known for its retro vibe, Talad Rot Fai features vintage clothing, antiques, and quirky decor items. This night market has an upbeat atmosphere with street food, live music, and a fun mix of vintage and modern shopping.

- **Location:** Srinakarin Soi 51, near Seacon Square Srinakarin.
- **Visiting Tip:** Wear comfortable shoes, as the market is extensive, and there's a lot to explore.

What to Buy: Souvenirs, Local Crafts, and More

Bangkok is full of unique items that make perfect souvenirs. Here are some popular souvenirs and crafts to get:

- **Thai Silk:** Known for its quality, Thai silk is available in scarves, ties, or as fabric. *Jim Thompson* and *Chatuchak Market* are great places to find authentic Thai silk.

- **Handicrafts and Pottery:** Thai handicrafts, like hand-carved wooden items, ceramics, and pottery, make meaningful souvenirs. Look for these at markets like *Chatuchak* and *SookSiam at Iconsiam*.

- **Spa Products:** Coconut oil, herbal balms, and scented soaps are great for those looking to bring a piece of Thai relaxation home. These are available at malls, markets, and health stores.

- **Snacks and Spices:** Thai curry paste, dried fruits, and locally made snacks make excellent edible souvenirs. *Gourmet Market* at Siam Paragon and *Chatuchak* are good places to pick up these items.

Bargaining Tips and Shopping Etiquette

Bargaining is a common practice in Bangkok's markets, but there are a few tips to ensure a respectful and enjoyable experience:

- **Start Low but Be Reasonable:** Begin with an offer around 50-60% of the asking price and negotiate up from there. Most vendors expect some haggling, so don't be afraid to counteroffer, but avoid low-balling too aggressively.

- **Use Cash:** Cash is preferred in most markets, and vendors may be more flexible with discounts when you pay in cash rather than with cards.

- **Be Polite:** Maintaining a friendly attitude goes a long way. Thais appreciate politeness, and smiling during negotiations can help achieve a better price.

- **Know When to Walk Away:** If you're not satisfied with the price, politely thank the vendor and walk away. They may offer a final discount, but if not, you can find similar items elsewhere.

- **Respect the Setting:** While bargaining is expected at markets, it's not appropriate in shopping malls or high-end stores, where prices are fixed.

From luxury malls to bustling street markets, Bangkok's shopping scene is diverse and exhilarating. Whether you're searching for high-end fashion or unique Thai souvenirs, the city offers countless opportunities to shop, explore, and take a piece of Bangkok home with you.

CHAPTER ELEVEN

Suggested Itineraries

Bangkok offers a wealth of experiences for every type of traveler, from cultural and historical sites to bustling markets, tranquil parks, and scenic riverside spots. Whether you're here for a day, a week, or looking for a family-friendly or romantic experience, these itineraries will help you make the most of your time in this dynamic city.

One-Day Itinerary: A Complete Experience

Morning

- **Grand Palace and Wat Phra Kaew:** Start your day at the iconic Grand Palace and *Wat Phra Kaew* (Temple of the Emerald Buddha) on *Na Phra Lan Road,* a must-see for any Bangkok visitor. The complex opens at 8:30 AM, so arriving early helps avoid the crowds.

- **Wat Pho:** Just a short walk from the Grand Palace, Wat Pho is home to the massive Reclining Buddha. Take time to explore the temple's intricate architecture and even indulge in a traditional Thai massage here.

Afternoon

- **Lunch at Thip Samai Pad Thai:** Known as one of Bangkok's best Pad Thai spots, *Thip Samai* is just a quick tuk-tuk ride away from Wat Pho. Enjoy a flavorful Pad Thai before continuing your journey.

- **Chao Phraya River Cruise:** Take a riverboat ride from *Tha Tien Pier* to see Bangkok from the water, passing sights like Wat Arun and other riverside temples.

Evening

- **Dinner and Shopping at Asiatique The Riverfront:** This riverside market offers dining, shopping, and entertainment. Enjoy dinner at one of the open-air restaurants, browse boutique shops, and take a ride on the Ferris wheel for views of the city at night.

Three-Day Itinerary: Exploring the City's Highlights in a Short Trip

A three-day stay allows you to dive deeper into Bangkok's major attractions and explore more of the city's dynamic neighborhoods. Below are suggested itineraries for a complete three-day experience:

Day 1: Historic and Cultural Landmarks

- **Morning:** Begin with the Grand Palace and *Wat Phra Kaew*, then head to *Wat Pho* to explore the temple grounds.

- **Afternoon:** Cross the river to visit *Wat Arun* (Temple of Dawn), known for its stunning riverside views and intricate porcelain decorations.

- **Evening:** Enjoy dinner at a riverside restaurant like *The Deck* for scenic views of Wat Arun illuminated at night.

Day 2: Modern Bangkok and Shopping

- **Morning:** Start your day at *Chatuchak Weekend Market* (if it's the weekend). This massive market is perfect for shopping for souvenirs, clothing, and handicrafts.

- **Afternoon:** Explore Bangkok's high-end shopping scene at *Siam Paragon* or

ICONSIAM, where you can browse luxury brands and boutique stores.

- **Evening:** Visit *Sky Bar at Lebua* for cocktails with a view of Bangkok's skyline. Dress smart-casual, as many rooftop bars have a dress code.

Day 3: Cultural Experiences and Relaxation

- **Morning:** Discover *Bang Krachao,* Bangkok's "Green Lung". Rent a bike and explore the area's lush surroundings and quiet roads, far removed from city noise.

- **Afternoon:** Head back to the city for a Thai massage at a reputable spa like *Let's Relax* or *Health Land.*

- **Evening:** Wrap up with dinner at *Soi 38 Sukhumvit*, a popular street food destination.

Seven-Day Bangkok Itinerary: A Complete Week of Adventure, Relaxation, and Culture

This week-long itinerary allows you to fully immerse yourself in Bangkok's culture, history, and modern lifestyle. Below are suggested itineraries for a complete seven-day experience:

Day 1: Historic Temples

Take a tour and have an eventful exploration of the Grand Palace, *Wat Phra Kaew*, *Wat Pho*, and *Wat Arun*. This full day of temple visits gives you an insight into Bangkok's rich heritage.

Day 2: Local Markets and Food

Spend the day exploring *Chatuchak Market* (on the weekend) or *Or Tor Kor Market* for fresh produce and authentic Thai snacks. In the evening, wander through *Yaowarat* for a memorable Chinatown street food experience.

Day 3: Museums and Art

Visit *Jim Thompson House*, then head to the *Bangkok National Museum* for Thai art and history.

Conclude with a visit to *MOCA Bangkok* (Museum of Contemporary Art) to see local contemporary artworks.

Day 4: Riverside Relaxation

Start your day with a boat ride on the *Chao Phraya River*. Later, explore *ICONSIAM* for shopping and riverside dining.

Day 5: Nature and Parks

Spend a day at *Lumphini Park* for relaxation and people-watching. In the afternoon, go to *Bang Krachao* for biking in Bangkok's "Green Lung".

Day 6: Day Trip to Ayutthaya

Take a day trip to *Ayutthaya*, the ancient capital of Siam, where you can explore the ruins of temples and palaces.

Day 7: Spa Day and Farewell Dinner

Treat yourself to a full spa day with traditional Thai treatments, and wrap up your week with a farewell dinner at *Baan Khanitha*, known for its refined Thai cuisine.

Three-Day Nature Lover's Itinerary: A Focus on Bangkok's Outdoors and Wildlife

For nature enthusiasts, Bangkok has many green spaces, parks, and eco-experiences. Below are suggested itineraries for a complete three-day outdoors and wildlife experience:

Day 1: Bang Krachao

- **Morning:** Rent a bike and explore Bang Krachao's lush forests, gardens, and bike trails.

- **Afternoon:** Have lunch at a local riverside café and visit the Bang Nam Phueng Floating Market on weekends.

- **Evening:** Return to Bangkok and have dinner in Sukhumvit.

Day 2: Parks and Gardens

- **Morning:** Visit Lumphini Park for a morning walk, or rent a paddleboat to enjoy the lake.

- **Afternoon:** Explore the Botanical Gardens within *Queen Sirikit Park*, near Chatuchak.
- **Evening:** Have your dinner at *EmQuartier*, enjoying the green surroundings of the *Helix dining zone*.

Day 3: Wildlife and River Views

- **Morning:** Visit *Safari World* on the outskirts of Bangkok, a popular park featuring a safari drive, marine park, and animal shows.
- **Afternoon:** Take a scenic boat ride along the *Chao Phraya River* and spot river wildlife.
- **Evening:** Enjoy dinner at a riverside restaurant to wrap up your nature-focused trip.

Three-Day Romantic Getaway Itinerary

If you're visiting Bangkok for a romantic escape, this itinerary includes stunning views, intimate dinners, and spa experiences.

Day 1: Romantic Views and Rooftop Dining

- **Morning:** Begin with a relaxing couple's spa treatment at a high-end spa like *Anantara* or *Banyan Tree*.

- **Afternoon:** Enjoy a peaceful afternoon walk in *Benjakitti Park*, followed by lunch in the area.

- **Evening:** Have a romantic dinner at *Vertigo* and *Moon Bar at Banyan Tree* for panoramic city views.

Day 2: Exploring Thai Culture Together

- **Morning:** Visit the Grand Palace and Wat Pho to explore Bangkok's history together.

- **Afternoon:** Have lunch near Wat Arun, then cross the river to explore the temple.
- **Evening:** Take a sunset cruise along the Chao Phraya River, enjoying dinner on board.

Day 3: Shopping and Relaxation

- **Morning:** Spend the morning shopping at Siam Paragon or Central Embassy for some upscale finds.
- **Afternoon:** Return for another spa session or enjoy the afternoon at your hotel pool.
- **Evening:** Have a private, intimate dinner at a cozy restaurant like Sühring or Paste, known for their romantic ambiance and exceptional cuisine.

Family Fun Itinerary: Tailored for Families Looking for Relaxation and Adventure

Bangkok offers a variety of family-friendly activities that both kids and adults can enjoy. Below are suggested itineraries for a complete family fun and relaxation experience:

Day 1: Iconic Attractions and Fun

- **Morning**: Explore the Grand Palace and Wat Pho for a family-friendly cultural experience.
- **Afternoon:** Visit *SEA LIFE Bangkok Ocean World i*n Siam Paragon, where kids can enjoy interactive marine exhibits.
- **Evening:** Dine at one of the family-friendly restaurants within Siam Paragon.

Day 2: Outdoor and Wildlife Activities

- **Morning:** Head to *Safari World* for a wildlife experience that the kids will love.

- **Afternoon:** Enjoy lunch at *Safari World*, then continue exploring the wildlife.
- **Evening:** Return to central Bangkok and have dinner near *Lumphini Park*, followed by a relaxed evening stroll.

Day 3: Shopping and Kid-Friendly Entertainment

- **Morning:** Explore Chatuchak Market for unique finds and snacks for the whole family.
- **Afternoon:** Head to *Terminal 21*, where the themed floors and food court offer fun for everyone.
- **Evening:** Finish the trip with a river dinner cruise, which offers great views and entertainment suitable for kids.

These itineraries provide a range of options to experience Bangkok based on different interests, whether you're on a tight schedule or have time to fully immerse yourself in the city's culture, nature, or romance. With this guide, you can create memorable moments tailored to your travel style, making the most of Bangkok's diverse offerings.

CHAPTER TWELVE

Practical Travel Information

Bangkok is an exciting and dynamic destination, but like any major city, being prepared with essential travel information can enhance your experience. Here's what you need to know about staying safe and healthy, staying connected, and handling finances while you're in the Thai capital.

Health and Safety Tips

- **Stay Hydrated and Protected from the Sun:** Bangkok's tropical climate can be challenging for travelers, especially those not used to the heat and humidity. Drink plenty of water, wear sunscreen, and take breaks in shaded areas or air-conditioned spaces. Bottled water is readily available at convenience stores throughout the city.

- **Food Safety:** Bangkok's street food is delicious, however, if you're new to Thai food, start with stalls that have a high turnover rate, as they're likely to have fresh ingredients. If you have a sensitive stomach, avoid raw or undercooked dishes and use hand sanitizer before meals.

- **Mosquito Protection:** Dengue fever and other mosquito-borne illnesses are present in Bangkok, though cases are relatively rare in urban areas. It's still wise to apply insect repellent, especially in parks or riverside areas. Wear long sleeves and pants in the evenings if you're spending time outdoors.

- **Road Safety:** Bangkok's roads can be chaotic, especially for pedestrians. Use crosswalks and follow local traffic signals. When taking motorbike taxis, ask for a helmet for safety. For short distances, the *BTS Skytrain* or *MRT subway* are safe and efficient options.

- **Respect Local Customs:** Thai culture values politeness, so avoid confrontation and maintain a respectful attitude. Follow dress codes when visiting temples and remove your shoes before entering sacred spaces or private homes.

Emergency Contacts and Medical Facilities

In case of emergency, Bangkok has a range of services and reputable hospitals with English-speaking staff to assist international visitors.

Emergency Numbers

- **Police:** 191.

- **Tourist Police:** 1155 (available 24/7 for tourist-related issues).

- **Ambulance and Medical Emergency**: 1669.

- **Tourist Police:** The Tourist Police are a helpful resource for foreign visitors. They can assist with lost belongings, safety concerns, and other travel-related issues. English-speaking officers are available, and they're familiar with handling issues specific to tourists.

Medical Facilities

Bangkok is home to some of Asia's top medical facilities, and many hospitals are equipped to handle foreign patients. The following are some of the top hospitals in Bangkok:

- **Bumrungrad International Hospital:** Located at Sukhumvit Soi 3, Watthana District, this world-renowned hospital is known for its high-quality care and international services, with English-speaking staff and translators available.

- **Bangkok Hospital:** Located at New Phetchaburi Road, Huai Khwang District, *Bangkok Hospital* offers specialized medical services, with a dedicated International Medical Center catering to foreign patients.

- **Samitivej Sukhumvit Hospital:** Located at Sukhumvit Soi 49, Watthana District, Samitivej is known for its family-oriented services, making it a good choice for travelers with children.

- **Pharmacies:** Pharmacies are widely available in Bangkok, with large chains like *Boots* and *Watsons* carrying a range of medications. You'll find English-speaking pharmacists in many locations, especially in tourist areas.

Communication: SIM Cards, WiFi, and Connectivity

Staying connected in Bangkok is easy, with various options for mobile data, WiFi, and SIM cards. Below are some of the things to put in mind as regards this aspect:

- **SIM Cards:** Upon arrival at *Suvarnabhumi* or *Don Mueang* airports, you'll find kiosks from major mobile providers like *AIS*, *TrueMove*, and *Dtac* offering prepaid SIM cards for tourists. Most packages include unlimited data, with options ranging from three to 30 days. Prices start at around 299 THB ($8) for a one-week package. Simply bring your passport, and the staff can set up the SIM card for you.

- **WiFi:** Bangkok has free WiFi in many public areas, including malls, cafes, and hotels. Major shopping centers like *Siam Paragon* and *CentralWorld* offer free WiFi for visitors. However, if you plan to be on the go, a local SIM card with mobile data is often more reliable.

- **Internet Cafes:** Although less common in the smartphone age, internet cafes can still be found in some areas and are useful if you need computer access.

- **Apps for Travel:** Downloading apps like Grab (for ride-sharing), Google Maps (for directions), and Translate (for language assistance) can be very helpful for navigating Bangkok with ease.

Money Matters: Currency, ATMs, and Tipping Culture

Understanding Bangkok's currency and handling finances in the city is simple with a few tips.

- **Currency:** Thailand's currency is the Thai Baht. Banknotes come in denominations of 20, 50, 100, 500, and 1,000 THB, while coins are available in 1, 2, 5, and 10 THB. It's wise to carry some small bills for taxis, street food, and small purchases, as not all vendors have change for larger notes.

- **ATMs:** ATMs are widely available in Bangkok, especially near shopping centers, tourist attractions, and convenience stores like *7-Eleven*. Most ATMs accept international cards but charge a fee (usually around 220 THB or $6.20) per transaction. To avoid multiple fees, consider withdrawing a larger amount at once. Notify your bank of your travel plans before using your card abroad to prevent any security issues.

- **Currency Exchange:** Exchange counters are easy to find in tourist areas and airports. *SuperRich* and *Vasu Exchange* are well-known for offering competitive rates. It's recommended to compare rates at different locations, as airport rates may be slightly less favorable.

Tipping Culture

Tipping in Thailand is not obligatory, but it's appreciated for good service. Here are general guidelines:

- **Restaurants**: In high-end restaurants or hotels, a 10% tip is appreciated, especially if no service charge is included in the bill. In casual eateries, rounding up the bill is often enough.

- **Hotels**: Bellhops and housekeeping staff typically receive a small tip of 20–50 THB ($0.60–$1.50).

- **Taxis**: While drivers don't expect tips, rounding up to the nearest 5–10 baht is common.

- **Street Vendors and Markets:** Tipping isn't expected, though leaving small change for excellent service is a nice gesture.

Cash vs. Card Payments

While most larger establishments accept credit cards, it's still common to use cash for small vendors, street food, and local markets. If you prefer to use a credit card, Visa and Mastercard are widely accepted, but be prepared with cash in smaller establishments.

Bangkok is a fantastic city for exploration, but knowing practical details ahead of time can make your trip more enjoyable and stress-free. With these travel tips, you'll be ready to handle health, connectivity, finances, and local etiquette, allowing you to immerse yourself fully in the Bangkok experience.

CHAPTER THIRTEEN

Sustainable and Responsible Travel

Bangkok, like many major cities, is working to balance rapid urban growth with sustainability. As a visitor, practicing responsible tourism and embracing eco-friendly activities can help support these efforts and preserve Bangkok's cultural and natural beauty for future generations. Here's how to explore Bangkok in an environmentally conscious and respectful way.

Eco-Friendly Activities

Bangkok offers plenty of eco-friendly activities that allow you to enjoy the city while minimizing your environmental footprint. Below are some of the top eco-friendly activities in Bangkok:

Explore Bang Krachao

Located across the Chao Phraya River in Phra Pradaeng, Bang Krachao is a lush, forested area. Renting a bike and exploring the mangroves, floating markets, and tranquil parks is recommended. It's a peaceful escape from the busy city and an excellent example of local conservation efforts.

Take the River Ferry

Instead of taking taxis or tuk-tuks, use the Chao Phraya River ferry system to reach riverside destinations like *Wat Arun* and *ICONSIAM*. Ferries are efficient, affordable, and emit less pollution than road vehicles. You'll enjoy a scenic view of the city's landmarks while reducing your environmental impact.

Visit Eco-Conscious Attractions

The *Jim Thompson House* and the *Bangkok Art and Culture Centre (BACC)* are two attractions that focus on preserving Thai art and culture. The Jim Thompson House supports local artisans, while BACC promotes sustainable and eco-friendly art exhibitions.

Eat at Farm-to-Table Restaurants

Dining at restaurants with farm-to-table or organic concepts supports local farmers and reduces the environmental impact of food transport. Some notable options include *Bo.lan*, which emphasizes sustainability, and *Err*, which focuses on local, seasonal ingredients.

Respectful and Ethical Tourism in Bangkok

Responsible tourism involves respecting local customs, supporting local businesses, and being mindful of ethical considerations. Below are some key points to put into consideration:

Be Mindful in Temples and Sacred Sites

Bangkok's temples are beautiful but also sacred spaces. Dress modestly, keep your voice low, and avoid taking intrusive photos of people praying. Always remove your shoes when entering temple buildings, and avoid pointing your feet toward Buddha statues or people.

Support Fair Trade and Local Artisans

When shopping, choose products from fair-trade shops or buy directly from local artisans at markets like *Chatuchak* or *ICONCRAFT* at *ICONSIAM*. By supporting local craftsmanship, you help sustain traditional skills and provide fair wages to artisans.

Avoid Exploitative Wildlife Tourism

Thailand is home to a wide array of wildlife, but not all attractions treat animals ethically. Avoid venues that offer elephant rides, tiger encounters, or other unnatural activities. Instead, support sanctuaries that focus on animal welfare, such as the *Wildlife Friends Foundation Thailand* in Phetchaburi or the *Elephant Nature Park* in Chiang Mai, both of which focus on rescue and rehabilitation.

Tips for Reducing Environmental Impact

Reducing your environmental footprint while traveling in Bangkok can be easy with a few mindful choices.

Opt for Public Transportation

Bangkok has an excellent public transportation network. The BTS Skytrain, MRT subway, and river ferries are efficient and environmentally friendly options for getting around. Avoid single-use taxi trips where possible and explore on foot if you're in a pedestrian-friendly area.

Bring a Reusable Water Bottle

Thailand's heat makes staying hydrated a priority, but instead of buying single-use plastic bottles, carry a reusable water bottle. Many hotels and cafes in Bangkok offer filtered water refilling stations, allowing you to cut down on plastic waste.

Limit Plastic Bags and Packaging

When shopping, refuse plastic bags by bringing a reusable tote. Bangkok's markets, in particular, are known for excess packaging, so kindly decline plastic bags when you can. It's a simple way to reduce waste and promote sustainable practices.

Stay at Eco-Friendly Accommodation

Bangkok has a growing selection of eco-friendly accommodations, like the *Bangkok Tree House* in Bang Krachao, which uses solar power and sustainable materials. Choosing a green-certified hotel can help support sustainable hospitality practices in Bangkok.

By embracing sustainable and responsible travel practices, you can enjoy Bangkok's dynamic culture while minimizing your impact on the environment and supporting ethical tourism. Small actions, like choosing public transportation, respecting local customs, and supporting fair-trade vendors, collectively contribute to preserving Bangkok for generations to come.

CHAPTER FOURTEEN

Useful Apps, Resources and Contacts

Planning a smooth and enjoyable trip to Bangkok requires knowing the best travel apps, reliable contact points, and trustworthy online resources. This chapter offers a carefully curated selection of essential apps, official tourism contacts, emergency information, and recommended websites that provide insights into Bangkok's culture, attractions, and travel logistics.

Essential Travel Apps for Bangkok

Bangkok is a large, bustling city, and these apps can help you explore it with ease, from finding transport options to checking out restaurant reviews.

Google Maps

Ideal for navigating Bangkok's bustling streets, Google Maps offers real-time traffic updates, walking directions, and public transportation routes, covering the BTS, MRT, and bus systems.

- **Website:** https://maps.google.com.

Grab

Grab is Bangkok's most popular ride-hailing app, offering transport options such as taxis, private cars, and motorbikes, along with food delivery services. It's a nice alternative to traditional taxis.

- **Website:** https://www.grab.com.

Line

Line is the most popular messaging app in Thailand, widely used for communication, including by many businesses for reservations and inquiries. If you plan to interact with locals or book tours through small operators, having Line can be very helpful.

- **Website:** https://line.me/en/.

Eatigo

Known for dining deals and discounts of up to 50% at popular Bangkok restaurants, Eatigo allows you to explore local cuisine on a budget.

- **Website:** https://eatigo.com/.

XE Currency

Xe Currency is ideal for quick currency conversions, especially useful for understanding prices in Thai Baht. It's constantly updated, ensuring that you always get the latest exchange rates.

- **Website:** https://www.xe.com.

Google Translate

Overcoming language barriers is easy with Google Translate, which includes text, voice, and camera translation options for Thai.

- **Website:** https://translate.google.com/.

BTS Skytrain and MRT Apps

Bangkok's *BTS Skytrain* and *MRT* have their own dedicated apps, providing real-time schedules, route maps, and fare calculators. These apps make navigating the city's trains simple and help you choose the quickest routes between attractions.

- **Website:** *BTS Skytrain:* https://www.bts.co.th/eng/

- *Bangkok MRT:* https://www.bemplc.co.th/.

Viabus

Viabus is perfect for those exploring Bangkok by bus, offering real-time bus locations, routes, and stops to keep your travels organized.

- **Website:** https://www.viabus.co/.

Klook / Viator

These apps offer tour and activity bookings in Bangkok, from cooking classes to temple visits, making it easy to plan and book experiences on the go.

- **Website:** *Klook*: https://www.klook.com.
- **Viator:** https://www.viator.com.

AirVisual

AirVisual tracks air quality in Bangkok, allowing you to plan outdoor activities on days with optimal conditions.

- **Website:** https://www.iqair.com/.

Official Tourist Information and Visitor Contacts

For accurate, up-to-date travel information, these official tourism contacts are invaluable resources:

Tourism Authority of Thailand (TAT)

TAT provides comprehensive information on Thailand's regions, cities, and attractions, including events, festivals, and local news. It's a useful resource for any traveler wanting a thorough overview of Bangkok and beyond.

- **Website:**

  https://www.tourismthailand.org/home.

Bangkok Tourism Division

This organization provides information on Bangkok's events, festivals, and local attractions, ideal for in-depth trip planning.

- **Address:** 17 Dinso Road, Sao Chingcha, Phra Nakhon, Bangkok 10200.

- **Website:** https://visit.bangkok.go.th/.

Tourist Information Centers

Found in high-traffic areas like Suvarnabhumi Airport and the Bangkok Art and Culture Centre, these centers offer brochures, maps, and staff assistance to answer tourist questions.

- **Location:** Available at major transport hubs and tourist attractions.

These offices provide local support, ensuring that your visit to Bangkok is as enjoyable and informative as possible.

Emergency and Embassy Contacts

Knowing emergency numbers and embassy contacts is essential for a safe and secure journey. Here are key contacts to keep handy:

Emergency Services

- **Police:** Dial 191.

- **Tourist Police**: Dial 1155 (English-speaking officers for tourist support).

- **Ambulance and Medical Emergencies:** Dial 1669.

- **Fire Department:** Dial 199.

Major Embassies

United States Embassy

The U.S. Embassy offers support and consular services for American citizens traveling in Thailand.

- **Phone:** +66 2 205 4000.

- **Website:** https://th.usembassy.gov/.

British Embassy

The British Embassy provides travel information and assistance for U.K. citizens visiting Bangkok.

- **Phone:** +66 2 305 8333.

- **Website:**
  https://www.gov.uk/world/organisations/britis h-embassy-bangkok.

Australian Embassy

Known for its comprehensive support services for Australian travelers, including passport assistance.

- **Phone:** +66 2 344 6300.

- **Website:** https://thailand.embassy.gov.au/.

Canadian Embassy

The Canadian Embassy offers essential services to Canadian citizens, including emergency assistance.

- **Phone:** +66 2 646 4300.

- **Website:** https://www.international.gc.ca/

Ireland Embassy

The *Embassy of Ireland in Thailand,* located in Bangkok, serves Irish citizens visiting or residing in Thailand, providing services such as passport renewals, consular assistance, and information on visas for travel to Ireland.

- **Phone:** +66 2 016 1360.
- **Website:**
  https://www.ireland.ie/en/thailand/bangkok/.

Recommended Websites and Blogs

For updated information, local insights, and travel tips, the following websites and blogs are trusted resources for Bangkok visitors:

Bangkok Tourism Guide

An independent guide that provides detailed information on Bangkok's attractions, accommodations, and dining spots.

- **Website:** https://www.bangkoktourismguide.com/.

Time Out Bangkok

It covers everything from local events to dining and nightlife, making it a go-to source for staying updated on Bangkok's social scene.

- **Website:** https://www.timeout.com/bangkok.

Bangkok Post

As one of Thailand's major English-language newspapers, the Bangkok Post covers news, events, and local issues. It's a reliable source for keeping up with what's happening around the city.

- Website: https://www.bangkokpost.com/.

The Thaiger

An engaging platform that offers the latest on Thai news, travel insights, and local events across Bangkok and Thailand.

- **Website:** https://thethaiger.com/

Nomadic Matt's Travel Blog – Bangkok

Nomadic Matt offers practical budget travel tips and recommendations for Bangkok, from attractions to local dining.

- **Website**: https://www.nomadicmatt.com/travel-guides/thailand-travel-tips/bangkok/

Coconuts Bangkok

Coconuts Bangkok covers Bangkok's local news, culture, and lifestyle. It's a great way to stay updated on current events and gain a deeper understanding of Thai culture.

- **Website:** https://coconuts.co/bangkok

Bangkok.com

Bangkok.com offers city guides for travelers, including the best places to eat, stay, and explore. The site covers a range of budgets, from luxury hotels to budget-friendly activities.

- **Website:** https://www.bangkok.com

By utilizing these apps, emergency contacts, and trusted websites, you'll be equipped with everything you need for a safe, connected, and well-informed journey through Bangkok. Whether you're navigating the city, finding local eateries, or staying updated on current events, these resources help make your trip seamless and enriching.

CONCLUSION

As your journey through this book comes to an end, your adventure in Bangkok is just beginning. This dynamic city, with its rich layers of history, culture, and modern energy, awaits you with open arms. From the bustling streets of *Chatuchak Market* to the peaceful serenity of *Lumphini Park*, Bangkok offers experiences that go beyond the pages and come to life in unforgettable moments.

Each chapter of this book has aimed to peel back the layers of this captivating city, revealing the treasures that make Bangkok so much more than just a travel destination. Traveling to Bangkok isn't just about seeing new sights; it's about connecting with a place that pulses with warmth, resilience, and tradition. Whether you're tasting the flavors of Thai street food, gazing at the shimmering spires of *Wat Arun*, or finding peace along the canals of *Bang Krachao*, each experience is an invitation to understand the soul of this remarkable city. Every interaction with Bangkok's people, each step through its markets, temples, and neighborhoods, will deepen your appreciation for its complexity and beauty.

As you explore, remember the principles of responsible travel and the importance of cultural respect. Traveling mindfully helps preserve Bangkok's charm for generations to come, ensuring that future visitors can experience the same magic.

Bangkok is more than a destination; it's a journey into the heart of Thailand. May your time here be filled with wonder, joy, and lasting memories. Thank you for bringing this book along on your journey.

Now, with curiosity as your compass, step into the city and let Bangkok leave its imprint on your heart. Safe travels, and may this enchanting city bring you experiences and connections that will last a lifetime.

Made in the USA
Monee, IL
02 January 2025

75762946R00134